What the Bible Says About Salvation • 49

h. Psalm 50:10–12

i. Proverbs 8:14

j. Haggai 2:8

k. What do these verses say to you about God's ability to provide whatever you need in life, physically or spiritually?

2. From these two verses in Acts, what evidence do you find that God has bestowed part of His riches upon the whole human race?

a. Acts 14:17

b. Acts 17:24

c. What does Acts 17:27 suggest as one of the reasons for God's "general" grace being bestowed upon all?

d. What are some of the blessings you received from God even before you became a Christian?

e. How aware are non-Christians that they are the recipients of the riches of God? How much more thankful to Him were you after you became a Christian?

3. Read Colossians 3:1–4.

   a. What definition of a Christian does Paul use in verse 1?

   b. What should Christians be seeking? (verse 1)

   c. Who is the true object of our seeking? (verse 1)

   d. What does it mean to set your mind on things above? (verse 2)

e. List five things that would occupy the thoughts of a person whose mind is set on . . .

. . . things above	. . . things below
1.	1.
2.	2.
3.	3.
4.	4.
5.	5.

f. What sort of death is Paul referring to in verse 3?

g. How should that death make a difference in where our mind is focused?

h. When, in the future, will our thoughts be legitimately focused on things below? (verse 4)

i. Whether He is in _____ or on _____, our

   thoughts should be focused on _____.

j. How would you evaluate where your mind is "set" most of the time?

k. What correlation do you find in your life between worrying about physical matters on earth and your focus on Christ?

4. From Jesus' words in Matthew 6:19–20 and 19:21, state in one sentence where true riches are to be found—and why.

DID YOU KNOW?

The *New American Standard Dictionary* says a eulogy is a "laudatory speech or written tribute . . . high praise or commendation." We think of eulogies most often in terms of funerals when the deceased is (hopefully) spoken well of. Our English word "eulogy" comes from the Greek verb *eulogeo,* to speak well of or praise. Therefore, in Ephesians 1:3 Paul "speaks well of" God because of how He has blessed us with every spiritual blessing. A comparison would be a eulogy at the funeral of a fabulously wealthy person who showered his riches upon others. He or she would be well-spoken of indeed. How much more is God to be "eulogized" for the riches He has showered on us.

EIGHT SPIRITUAL BLESSINGS

Ephesians 1:3–14

In this lesson we discover eight spiritual blessings which belong to every Christian.

OUTLINE

Reading books surveying the Old and New Testaments is a helpful way for new Christians to learn the "big ideas" of the Bible. In the same way, the apostle Paul surveys and summarizes the infinite riches of God in Christ by summarizing them from eternity past to eternity future.

   I.   **Chosen**

  II.   **Adopted**

 III.   **Accepted**

 IV.   **Redeemed**

  V.   **Enlightened**

 VI.   **Obtained an Inheritance**

VII.   **Sealed**

VIII.   **Secured**

E phesians 1:3–14 is the longest sentence in the Bible. I recall having to diagram this sentence in Greek when in seminary, and the diagram ran off the page onto a second page because the sentence goes on and on. But this sentence is a picture of the blessings of God—they just keep going on and on.

Paul says in verse three that we have been blessed with every spiritual blessing, and in verses 4 through 14 he describes what those blessings are. When he began writing them down, I think he couldn't stop. He created the longest run-on sentence in the Bible as his mind raced from one blessing to the next. It may not be the best grammar, but it is the best summary in the Bible of the spiritual blessings we have in Christ.

He starts with blessings whose origin is in eternity past and finishes with blessings that end in eternity future. In between is a sequential description of the blessings the Christian enjoys between the two eternities. While there would be great value in spending an entire lesson on each of the eight blessings Paul mentions, we will cover them all in one lesson in an overview. Using that approach, we get a great appreciation for the totality of what God has done and Paul's purposes in grouping them together in succession.

CHOSEN (1:4)

We were chosen in Christ "before the foundation of the world, that we should be holy and without blame before Him in love."

Because God is love, and love always looks for others to love, He created for Himself a group of people with whom He would enjoy fellowship for eternity. And He chose them before they were ever created, even before the creation of the world.

The subject of God's choosing immediately raises questions of predestination and election—prickly topics among some in the body of Christ. But after a thorough study of the subject of God's choosing, I can safely tell you what it means: God chose us! If words have meaning (and they do), then that is what the Bible means when it says "He chose us in Him." No one can comprehend or explain how or why some were chosen and others were not. It is a mystery. All we can say is that God's choosing is a matter of His wisdom and grace—and rejoice if we find ourselves among the chosen.

The chosen are the "us" we discussed in the last lesson (verse 3)—all Christians who claim God as their Father and Christ as their

Lord and Savior. Being chosen has nothing to do with us. There is nothing any Christian did to influence God's choosing. In fact, we were chosen in spite of ourselves. We don't proclaim ourselves as chosen out of arrogance or pride, but rather humility. The only reason we mention it at all is that we would be unfaithful to Scripture if we didn't. God chose us because of His love, mercy, and grace.

ADOPTED (1:5)

God "predestined us to adoption as sons by Jesus Christ to Himself, according to the good pleasure of His will."

The word "predestined" means to set boundaries so that we stay on a certain course. God chose us, then predestined us—set boundaries around our lives so we would achieve a specific end: to become His sons and daughters. He chose us, then predestined us to be His adopted child.

One of my four children is adopted. Having gone through the adoption process, my wife and I deepened our understanding of what adoption means, at least from the perspective of raising a child that is not naturally yours. Our daughter became part of our family by a legal act, not by flesh and blood birth. While some of that is pictured in ancient adoptions, there was more involved in the biblical use of the term. In Greek families, you were considered a child until you reached a certain age, at which time you were established as a son in the family with all the rights and privileges of sonship. That idea is behind the biblical concept of adoption. God chose us and purposed that we should come into His family as mature sons and daughters and receive full status as His children.

Because we were adopted into God's family as mature sons and daughters, we have the same status with God as does Jesus Christ. We are heirs of God and co-heirs with Christ. When God looks at us, He doesn't see us; He sees us in Christ. The standing I have with God is because of Christ, not because of who I am. He chose us in Christ and made sure we reached the status of sons and daughters in His family.

ACCEPTED (1:6)

". . . to the praise of the glory of His grace, by which He made us accepted in the Beloved."

I could cite endless illustrations from our modern culture of the extent to which people go to gain acceptance. Fads, fashion, finances and more are means to the end of acceptance in our society.

Everyone is on a quest to be accepted. Did you know that all the major religions of the world are just efforts by people to gain acceptance by Almighty God? Even within Christianity, there are those who believe their works will make them acceptable to God. But the problem is that we can never do enough. Because God's standard is perfection, we are on an endless journey to reach that state ourselves, which, of course, we can never do. We can never find acceptance with God so long as it depends on our own imperfect efforts.

"Beloved" in this passage refers to the Lord Jesus Christ. At His baptism and again on the Mount of Transfiguration, God called Jesus His "beloved Son" (Matthew 3:17; 17:5). If Jesus is God's beloved Son, and we are adopted in Christ into God's family, then how does God see us? As beloved in Jesus Christ. We have been "accepted in the Beloved."

The English hymn writer Catesby Paget reflected this truth in verse:

Near, so very near to God,
Nearer I cannot be;
For in the person of his Son
I am as near as he.
So dear, so very dear to God,
More dear I cannot be;
The love wherewith he loves the Son—
Such is his love to me.

A story from the Civil War is told about a Union soldier who went to the White House hoping to see President Lincoln. While waiting in a room filled with people who also wanted to see the president, a small boy wandered over to the soldier and struck up a conversation. When the soldier told the boy his mission, the boy told him his name—it was Tad Lincoln. He promised the soldier the president would see him. Eventually the president's secretary came and dismissed all who were waiting, saying the president couldn't see any more people that day. Everyone left except the soldier, who told the secretary that the president's son had assured him he would see the president. The secretary assured the soldier that if the president's son asked the president to see him, then the president would indeed see him.

I'm like that soldier. I want to be seen (accepted) by God, but I can't get there on my own. But because I know God's Son and am ushered into God's presence by His own Son, I become accepted by the Father. To be accepted in the beloved means to gain acceptance with God because of the merits of Jesus Christ.

Redeemed (1:7)

"In Him we have redemption through His blood, the forgiveness of sins, according to the riches of His grace."

There is one simple reason why we need to be redeemed: we are sinners! Paul describes our need for redemption in Ephesians 2:1–3, saying we were "dead in trespasses and sins." No one can read that passage and come away thinking mankind doesn't need to be redeemed.

The word "redemption" refers to buying back or setting free. The picture is that we were slaves to sin before knowing Christ. And the only way we could be free is for someone to buy us out of slavery; to redeem us and set us free. And that is what Christ did through the purchase price of His own blood.

While visiting in a certain city once, I was told to be sure and visit the site of the old slave market which still existed from the nineteenth century. As I walked through that market, I had the ominous feeling that comes when you visit someplace where something really bad took place. In this case, it was a place where precious human beings were bought and sold as property. But it also made me remember that Christ purchased us out of slavery to sin—redeemed us for a new and different life.

The result of redemption is forgiveness of sins. We could not have been purchased from the marketplace of sin unless our sins had been paid for, which they were by the blood of Christ. I pray that you have experienced being redeemed and that you know the blessed state of having all your sins forgiven.

Enlightened (1:8–9)

"... having made known to us the mystery of His will, according to His good pleasure which He purposed in Himself."

As a result of being chosen, adopted, accepted, and redeemed, God gives us a new sense of understanding about Him and about life. The riches of His grace abound toward us "in all wisdom and prudence." Wisdom is understanding the deep things of God and prudence is knowing how to apply them in your life.

The Bible says that "the natural man does not receive the things of the Spirit of God, for they are foolishness to him; nor can he know them, because they are spiritually discerned" (1 Corinthians 2:14).

I've had people tell me through the years that they can't understand the Bible, and that's why they're not going to become a Christian. With that reasoning, they will likely never be saved because only a person indwelt by the Spirit can truly understand the Word of God. But then God breaks into their life, they are saved by grace, and suddenly the Bible begins to make sense.

One of the blessings of God's riches is an enlightened mind by which we are able to understand the things of the Spirit of God. As a result, our understanding deepens not only about God but about the ways of God in His kingdom and in this world.

OBTAINED AN INHERITANCE (1:11-12)

"In Him also we have obtained an inheritance, being predestined according to the purpose of Him who works all things according to the counsel of His will."

As a result of becoming a child in the family of God, we gain all the rights and privileges of sonship, one of which is becoming an heir. As a son or daughter of God, we automatically qualify for an inheritance. We do not know exactly what the inheritance is going to be, but we know what the apostle Peter calls it: "an inheritance incorruptible and undefiled and that does not fade away, reserved in heaven for you" (1 Peter 1:3–4). Our inheritance is not going to be affected by world markets, by inflation, or by recession. It is an inheritance that thieves cannot steal nor moths nor rust destroy (Matthew 6:20).

You may occasionally read stories in the news about fabulous inheritances that are received by individuals in this world—and some of them are huge by human standards. But the largest of earthly inheritances pale in comparison to the inheritance God has planned for those who love Him (1 Corinthians 2:9).

SEALED (1:13)

After becoming a Christian, every believer is "sealed with the Holy Spirit of promise."

This is not just theological rhetoric or religious language; being sealed by the Holy Spirit is a specific act that occurs in time and space. The sealing by the Spirit refers to our security with God in the present. We know we were chosen by God in eternity past and we will be secure with God in eternity future. But what about in between? What security do I have that I am going to make it through this life faithfully, given the traps and pitfalls and snares that exist?

When we become Christians the Holy Spirit comes to live within us and serves as a deposit, or a guarantee, that we're going to make it. Think of what happens when you send a piece of registered mail. The post office employee puts a stamp, a kind of seal, on the outside of the letter. If anyone besides the designated recipient opens that letter, the seal will be broken. The seal is the guarantee that the letter gets where it is supposed to go.

In the same way the Holy Spirit is the guarantee that what God has promised in the past, He will fulfill in the future. The Spirit is the earnest, like a down payment, part of the inheritance which guarantees that God is going to give us all the rest. The Holy Spirit bears witness with our spirit that we are indeed God's child and that our inheritance is reserved in heaven (Romans 8:16).

SECURED (1:14)

The Holy Spirit is the "guarantee of our inheritance until the redemption of the purchased possession, to the praise of His glory."

The old King James Version refers to the Spirit in this verse as the "earnest" of our inheritance. Earnest was an old word for down payment, as in the "earnest money" that accompanies a contract offer to purchase a new home. When you put down earnest money, that means you guarantee to come back at the closing on the house with the rest of the money. If you don't, you forfeit the earnest money. Now God is not going to default on His promise to us to hand over the Holy Spirit! We can know that the Spirit is an infallible deposit, that God is going to make good on His promise to give us our full inheritance in heaven.

In light of this teaching, some will ask whether it is possible to lose one's salvation. All I can say is, to do that, I would have to undo God's choosing, His adopting, His accepting, His redeeming, His enlightening, His assigning of an inheritance, His sealing, and His securing of my life for all eternity. As I have heard it said before, I would have to undo what God thought, Jesus bought, and the Spirit wrought.

I believe the blessings and riches of God are so sure that I am His forever in spite of all my flaws, faults, and failures. As surely as I prepare these words for your instruction and edification in studying God's Word, I am sure I will be with Him forever. I hope you are sure of the same thing.

APPLICATION

1. Read Romans 9:6–21.

   a. What does Paul say about being a descendant of Abraham? (verses 6–8)

   b. How did God determine which of Isaac's twins—Jacob or Esau—would be the spiritual descendant of Abraham? (verses 10–13)

   c. What is and is not the basis of God's choosing? (verse 16)

   d. What is Paul's response to those who might question God's fairness in choosing? (verses 19–21)

   e. What should be the Christian's response to God's mercy-based choosing? (Romans 12:1)

2. Read Galatians 4:1–7.

   a. What was the status of a child in a Roman household? (verses 1–2)

   b. What was the Christian's status before being adopted into God's household? (verse 3)

c. What did God do to change our status? (verses 4–5)

d. What did God provide to give us a relationship with the Father? (verse 6)

e. How does our status change in Christ? (verse 7)

3. Read Romans 5:1–11.

a. What is the source of the access we now have to God? (verses 1–2)

b. What power did we have to gain access to God? (verse 6)

c. What is the only basis on which God would have accepted His enemies? (verse 10)

d. What should be the heart attitude of all who have been accepted by God? (verse 11)

4. Read Ephesians 1:7.

   a. What is the basis of our redemption? (verse 7a)

   b. What is the result of our redemption? (verse 7b)

   c. With what is our redemption consistent? (verse 7c)

5. Read 1 Corinthians 2:9–16.

   a. How have we come to know what we know of God? (verse 10)

   b. How are man's spirit and the Spirit of God compared by Paul? (verse 11)

   c. What chance does the man without the Spirit have of accepting the things of God? (verse 14)

d. Whose mind do we have? (verse 16)

6. Name those whom Paul says will not gain an inheritance from God: (Ephesians 5:5)

   a. In Colossians 3:24, Paul speaks of our inheritance as a reward. In what way does that change or expand the idea of an inheritance?

7. What do you learn about the Holy Spirit's role in the believer's life from the following verses?

   a. 2 Corinthians 1:22

   b. 2 Corinthians 5:5

   c. Romans 5:5

8. Contrast the difference in God being responsible for your eternal security versus you being responsible for your eternal security.

DID YOU KNOW?

Some scholars regard Ephesians 1:10 as a summary, or theme, verse for the whole epistle. There Paul talks about God's intent, in the fullness of time, to gather together everything in heaven and on earth in Christ. Paul uses an interesting word—*anakephalaioo*—which we translate "gather together." It is a word which has mathematical connotations: to add a column of figures, or to sum up. Its only other New Testament use is Romans 13:9, where Paul "sums up" a number of the Ten Commandments by the requirement to love one's neighbor as oneself. In Ephesians, Paul is saying that one day God is going to make everything total up correctly under the Lordship of Christ.

A Prayer to Empower Your Life

Ephesians 1:15–23

In this lesson we learn about the mighty power of God in Christ.

OUTLINE

Can you imagine a person receiving a letter in the mail informing him he was the winner of a contest, but never going to pick up the prize? If we never make the transition from head knowledge to heart knowledge in the Christian life, we would be just as foolish.

I. **The Occasion of Paul's Prayer**

II. **The Object of Paul's Prayer**
   A. The Priority of Knowing Christ
   B. The Possibility of Knowing Christ
   C. The Purpose of Knowing Christ

The home of the former and famous newspaper publisher William Randolph Hearst, known as Hearst Castle, is a prime tourist attraction on California's Central Coast. Besides being a tourist site, it is home to valuable pieces of art collected by Hearst from all over the world. Once when Hearst was reading an art catalog, he read a description of some valuable pieces which he immediately decided he had to have for his own collection. He commissioned his agent to find the pieces and add them to his collection, regardless of cost. You can imagine his surprise when he received a telegram from his art agent telling him the pieces had been located—they were in Hearst's own warehouse where his collection of art was stored!

If William Randolph Hearst had compared what he wanted with what he already possessed, he would have discovered that the very things he longed for were already his.

In the first two lessons in this study, we established from the opening verses of Ephesians that the Christian has been blessed with "every spiritual blessing" in Christ. We have been chosen, adopted, accepted, redeemed, enlightened, made an heir, sealed, and secured—all as part of God's riches of grace. The conclusion of chapter one (verses 15–23) is Paul's expression of desire that believers embrace and walk in the riches we have been provided in Christ. It is Paul's passionate prayer that we might move from head knowledge to heart knowledge in the Christian life. While verses 3–14 were a section of praise for God's provision, verses 15–23 are a prayer for the Ephesians (and for us) that we might walk in all that is ours by faith.

THE OCCASION OF PAUL'S PRAYER (1:15–16)

"Therefore" in Scripture is always a signpost telling us to determine what it is "there for." In this case, Paul's prayer is based directly on what he has just concluded in the preceding verses about the riches that are ours in Christ. "Since you have these riches," he is saying, "here is what I pray for you." The faith of the Ephesians, coupled with their love for fellow-saints, prompts Paul to record what he has been ceaselessly praying for them.

Paul has just taken them on an eternity-to-eternity survey of the riches that are theirs in Christ. The blessings of God began in eternity past and will continue in eternity future; and in between, there is nothing but blessing as well. Paul's recitation of these blessings turned into the longest continual sentence in the New Testament, a doxology of praise to God for what He has provided in Christ. Every Christian should respond with the same praise as Paul did when we consider what God has done.

Paul's prayer, one of two in Ephesians (see 3:14), has a particular motivation in the mind of the apostle. He knew it was possible to hear spiritual truth on an intellectual basis only. He knew that reading a list of blessings wasn't going to change anyone's life. It's very easy to get hardened to the truth, to develop calluses on the soul. Paul feared the Ephesians might develop a case of "So what?" after reading about their riches in Christ. Having faith, even having love, for which he commends them, is not enough. He wants them to walk in all of God's blessings and riches.

Someone said something to me recently that I'd never heard before. I wrote it down because of its significance: "On my way to the Savior, I ran into service." He meant that he got sidetracked from the best thing by a good thing. Service is good, but too much of it can keep us from the Savior. We don't know God primarily through service or ministry in spite of their value and necessity. We know God primarily by spending time with His Son. Many in full-time or vocational ministry know that their ministry can be an occupational hazard as on any other job. It can keep them from spending time with the Savior.

I read a story recently about a pastor who was touring the country speaking on prophecy, on matters concerning the end times. He had been doing it for years until one day he confessed to a friend that he had lost complete touch with how to be filled with the Holy Spirit. He had been so focused on his ministry that he had ignored the basics of the Christian life. Paul didn't want that to happen to the Ephesian Christians.

THE OBJECT OF PAUL'S PRAYER (1:17–19a)
The Priority of Knowing Christ (1:17)

The object of Paul's prayer, beginning in verse 17, is that Christians in Ephesus might know God better, that they would receive "the spirit of wisdom and revelation in the knowledge of Him."

There are three key words in this verse: wisdom, revelation, and knowledge. We have the Bible today because God revealed His words to those who then wrote them down. God, through revelation, deposited His words into the Bible by the Holy Spirit (2 Timothy 3:16;

2 Peter 1:20–21). Then, He gives us the Holy Spirit so the Bible can be revealed to our hearts, allowing us to understand it.

God wants us to go beyond a devotional reading of the Bible, even though there is value in that. He wants us to know Christ more deeply through reading His Word. He wants to reveal to us through His Word the infinite depths of His Son which only come through revelation. We can breeze through the Bible and never enter into the experience of revelation—when God speaks to us through His Word in a deep and life-changing way.

I know about the president of our country, but I don't know him personally. If I met him on the street, I would recognize him, but he wouldn't recognize me. That's how a lot of Christians know Christ—by name only, not on a personal basis. For them Christianity is a religion, not a relationship.

Paul was praying for the Ephesians something he prayed for himself: "that I may know Him and the power of His resurrection, and the fellowship of His sufferings, being conformed to His death" (Philippians 3:10). And that is what each of us should desire for ourselves: a constantly deepening walk with the Savior on the basis of wisdom, revelation, and knowledge.

The Possibility of Knowing Christ (1:18a)

The way we know Christ more deeply is by "the eyes of [our] understanding being enlightened." The word "understanding" is really the word "heart"—"the eyes of [our] heart being enlightened." The heart Paul refers to is not the organ that pumps our blood; it is the mind, emotions, and will combined, the seat of our knowledge and volition. The Holy Spirit comes in and shines a light of understanding (enlightens) in our mind, emotions, and will which translates into action.

Without the Holy Spirit, our hearts (our understanding) remain darkened (1 Corinthians 2:14). The natural man thinks Christians are pretty foolish to believe in someone they've never even seen. But then when that man becomes a Christian, he believes the same thing! Why? Because his understanding has been enlightened.

The Purpose of Knowing Christ (1:18–23)

Paul details three purposes for having our heart enlightened, for knowing Christ in a deep way—and they are three purposes you may never have considered. In verses 18 and 19, these three are all introduced by the word "what."

1. To know the prospect He has in store for us (1:18b)

   The first is to know "the hope of His calling"; that is, what God has in store for us. The word "hope" makes us think about the future, the fact that God didn't save us just to let us sit, soak, and sour. He saved us to a glorious hope!

   First John 3:2 says that when Christ comes again, "We shall be like Him, for we shall see Him as He is." Not only are we going to be *with* Jesus one day, we are going to be *like* Him as well—holy and blameless, without sin. That is part of the hope of our calling.

   First Corinthians 2:9 says that our senses cannot comprehend what God has prepared for those who love Him. That's why it has to be revealed to us by supernatural revelation. God begins to give us inklings in our spirit of what He has prepared for those He has called.

2. To know the pleasure He takes in us (1:18c)

   The second "what" is "the riches of the glory of His inheritance in the saints." This just blesses my heart! In the last lesson, we talked about our inheritance in Christ. But here, Paul says that we are God's inheritance. When Christ looks out over the world and sees the multitudes of those who believe in Him, He sees us as a special treasure, as His special inheritance. No Christian should struggle with self-esteem from God's perspective. He loves us so much that He views us as a worthy inheritance for His own Son. And Christ loved us enough to purchase us with the price of His own precious blood. That kind of love should be enough to establish a proper perspective on our value to God.

   Psalm 149 says "the Lord takes pleasure in His people" (verse 4). He takes pleasure in us because of the value we have in His sight, because He loved us enough to give His only Son for us. And that knowledge comes through revelation by the Spirit.

3. To know the power He can release in us (1:19–23)

   The final "what" is "the exceeding greatness of His power toward us who believe." Jesus Christ is the source of our power as Christians, and He wants His power to be released through you.

It grieves me when I see and hear Christians for whom the spiritual life is as much falling down as it is moving forward. I've never understood how that reflects the power of God through Christ living in us. All of us fall down at times, but I believe it should be less and less as we move deeper into our walk with Christ. When we do fall down, we should stay down shorter and get up quicker as we move forward.

Paul illustrates the power of Christ four ways in the remaining verses of this chapter:

a. The power of His resurrection (1:20a)

The same power that raised Christ from the dead is resident in those who know Christ. Paul uses the word *dunamis* to refer to power, the word from which we get "dynamite." Dynamite can do many things, but it can't raise the dead. But that is what the *dunamis* of God did in the resurrection of Christ. And that is the power of Christ that resides in us.

I recall reading how John D. Rockefeller, at one time the richest man in America, was consumed by fear that someone was going to steal his riches. He lived under constant stress until he discovered that philanthropy provided an avenue for using his wealth to benefit others. He initially had great riches but was powerless to enjoy them, and was miserable. God has given us a great inheritance; but without the power to use it, we will likewise be miserable.

b. The power of His ascension (1:20b)

Not only was the power of God present in Christ's resurrection, but in His ascension as well. Christ was seated "at [God's] right hand in the heavenly places." Jesus was brought out of the ground, back to ground level, then taken beyond that to heaven—and so have we if we are in Christ (Romans 6). We have experienced the same transforming power that raised Christ from the dead and seated Him in heavenly places. The question is whether we are availing ourselves of that power.

c. The power of His exultation (1:21–22)

Not only was Christ raised from the dead, seated at the right hand of God, but He has also been set above "all principality and power and might and dominion, and every name that is named, not only in this age but also in that which is to come." Jesus is above everyone and everything (Philippians 2:9–11)! He is the ultimate power in the universe and we are in Him!

Unfortunately, many live their lives here on earth as if they are stuck here, beholden to every human or spiritual power that comes along. In reality, we are in Christ who is above every power that exists. There is no reason for any Christian to live in defeat or fear. Satan and sin are defeated enemies and we live in the One who defeated them by His power. There is no problem or situation in life for which God's mighty power, given to us, is not adequate.

d. The power of His position (1:22b–23)

God's power in Christ is evident in the resurrection, the ascension, and the exaltation of Christ. Therefore, Christ's position is an obvious one: Everything is "under His feet" (Psalm 110:1). He is "head over all things to the church, which is His body, the fullness of Him who fills all in all." Not only is there power in Christ, there is authority by virtue of His position over all things. And to whom is His authority and power made available? To the church, the body of Christ. Christian, don't live without power! Christ has it all, and He has all you will ever need.

To conclude this lesson, allow me to make two points of application:

1. Given the kind of power that is available to all who believe in Christ, there is no sinner who is beyond being rescued by God. I've heard people say they are convinced they could never be saved because of the depth of their sins. But how do any of our sins measure up against the power that raised, ascended, exalted, and set Christ above all other powers— including the power of sin and its penalty? They do not. Christ is greater, and no sinner should feel himself beyond the reach of Christ's power to save (Hebrews 7:25a).

2. Not only is there no sinner beyond rescue, but there is no saint beyond recovery. Sometimes after being redeemed and forgiven, the life of a Christian gets messed up—he thinks he's blown it with God; he thinks there is no recovery. He acts like a person whom God has cured of cancer but who can't trust Him to heal his arthritis. God has already done the biggest thing by forgiving our sins, yet some people can't seem to trust Him to restore them when they stumble and fall. Christ's power is sufficient not only to rescue you, but to restore you no matter what you've done.

Join the Ephesians as the object of Paul's prayer and partake of the power of God in Christ.

APPLICATION

1. Read 2 Peter 1:19–21.

   a. How is the word of God characterized in verse 19?

   b. How is that characterization consistent with the revelation of truth in the human heart?

   c. From whence does Scripture originate? (verse 21)

   d. How were men moved to write the Bible? (verse 21)

   e. Therefore, revelation of the Word into the human realm is a

      function of the _____ _____.

2. Read 2 Timothy 3:16–17.

   a. How was Scripture given? (verse 16)

b. What assumption is made about man's "completeness" before receiving God's revelation of instruction? (verse 17)

c. What parallel can you draw between the revelation of the Word in the Bible and the revelation of the Word in the human heart?

3. Read Proverbs 2:1–8.

a. What verbs are used in verses 2–3 to describe the process of gaining wisdom, insight, and discernment?

b. What does the metaphor of mining for precious stones suggest about the process of gaining wisdom?

c. Who is the source of wisdom, knowledge, and understanding? (verse 6)

d. What do these verses suggest to you about how easy or difficult it is to gain wisdom?

e. If God doesn't provide it by revelation, how likely are we to attain it?

4. Read 1 Corinthians 1:18–31.

   a. What is the message of the Cross to those who don't believe? (verse 18)

   b. What is one of God's purposes in salvation? (verse 18)

   c. Why does the Gospel seem foolish to the natural man?

   d. What can the world know, through its own wisdom, about God? (verse 21)

   e. To the perishing Christ is _____ and _____,

      but to the Christian Christ is _____ and _____. (verses 23–24)

f. List the words used in verses 27–28 to describe "what" God chose to confound the wisdom of the world:

g. Which should Christians boast in: human wisdom or the revelation of God? (verse 31)

5. Read Romans 6:1–10. Identify the verses that discuss the Christian's identity with Christ's death, resurrection, and current reign.

   a. Death

   b. Resurrection

   c. Reign

   d. How closely identified with Christ's power is the believer?

6. What area(s) of your life have you wished God's power could change?

a. What does this study of the power of Christ in the believer suggest to you about His power to help?

b. What steps can you take to begin trusting God afresh to manifest the power of Christ in this area(s) of your life?

DID YOU KNOW?

The trilogy of New Testament virtues found in Ephesians 1:15, 18—faith, hope, and love—is most identified with Paul's words in 1 Corinthians 13:13. But they occur also in eight other New Testament passages (Romans 5:1–5; Galatians 5:5–6; Ephesians 4:2–5; Colossians 1:4–5; 1 Thessalonians 1:3; 5:8; Hebrews 6:10–12; 1 Peter 1:21–22). These three virtues, along with grace and truth (John 1:14, 17), "summarize the Gospel and its consequences" (*Ephesians* in the *NIV Application Commentary*, p. 71). All five terms—faith, hope, love, grace, and truth—occur in three important theological passages: Galatians 5:4–7; Ephesians 4:2–15; Colossians 1:4–6.

WHAT THE BIBLE SAYS ABOUT SALVATION

Ephesians 2:1–10

In this lesson we review the past, present, and future of our salvation.

OUTLINE

Where would you take someone in the Bible to give them a summary, an overview, of the Gospel—what salvation is all about. In Ephesians 2, Paul does just that. He reviews for the Christians in Ephesus why they were saved, how they were saved, and for what purpose.

I. **The Reason for Salvation: Past**
   A. We Were Dead
   B. We Were Deceived
   C. We Were Disobedient
   D. We Were Defiled
   E. We Were Doomed

II. **The Remedy of Salvation: Present**
   A. Rich Mercy
   B. Great Love
   C. Rich Grace
   D. Free Gift
   E. Through Faith

III. **The Result of Salvation: Future**
   A. For God
   B. For Man

I remember being captivated by watching the live television coverage of a mining accident in the coal mining region of the eastern United States. A group of miners was trapped below the surface, waiting helplessly as rescuers struggled to reach them from the surface. I remember watching with anguish when a huge drill bit broke that was being used to bore a shaft down to where the miners were trapped. That resulted in hours of delays as a replacement bit was located. All the while, I just kept thinking about what those miners were experiencing beneath the ground as the minutes ticked by.

Thinking back over that event since then (the miners were ultimately rescued), I've realized that the utter helplessness and hopelessness those trapped miners felt is an excellent picture of our lost condition. As lost sinners, alienated from God, we are helpless and hopeless. There is nothing we can do on our own to fix our situation. If we are going to be rescued it will be completely the result of God's efforts, not our own.

That is the message Paul has for the Ephesian church beginning in chapter two of his letter. In the first chapter, he talked about the riches of God's blessing and the power of God that has been revealed in Christ (and in us). He prayed that the Ephesians would come to realize "what is the exceeding greatness of His power toward us who believe, according to the working of His mighty power" (1:19). In chapter two he continues illustrating the power of God by presenting a "before and after" picture of the Christian.

The passage falls into three sections. First, the reason for salvation (our past); second, the remedy for salvation (our present); and third, the result of salvation (our future).

THE REASON FOR SALVATION: PAST (2:1–3)

Paul explains why we are not able to save ourselves; why we are not able, as other religions teach, to do whatever is necessary to earn the favor of God. There are five reasons.

We Were Dead (2:1)

First, we were dead "in trespasses and sins." This refers, of course, to spiritual, not physical, deadness, which means we are dead toward God. We cannot communicate with God because our spirits are dead and the Holy Spirit does not live within us. When we become Christians, our spirits are quickened (made alive) by the presence of the Holy Spirit and we are changed from death to life.

Ephesians 4:18 says our understanding was darkened, we were alienated from God, we were ignorant (about spiritual matters), and blind in our hearts. Being alienated from God is the bottom line, what it means to be spiritually dead. We have already seen in our study of Ephesians that the natural man cannot understand the things of God; spiritual matters seem foolish to a person who is dead spiritually.

The Bible says we were born in this condition, that we entered the world as spiritually dead beings. We like to think of tiny newborns as sweet and innocent beings, totally removed from the concept of sin and death. But they are as spiritually dead as the vilest sinful adult. They simply have not had time to exercise their sin nature, which every parent knows reveals itself all too soon. The psalmist David wrote, "Behold, I was brought forth in iniquity, and in sin my mother conceived me" (Psalm 51:5). He is not saying the sexual act that resulted in his conception was sinful. He is saying that when he was conceived and born, he was born into the realm of sin.

The word "trespasses" in Ephesians 2:1 has the same meaning as it does in a "No Trespassing" sign: "Don't cross this line." In the same way, when we trespass against God, we cross the line separating righteousness from unrighteousness. We disobey His "No Trespassing" sign and cross over into sin. And "sin" means to "miss the mark," to miss God's target of righteousness.

We Were Deceived (2:2a)

Because we were dead spiritually, we were deceived into walking "according to the course of this world, according to the prince of the power of the air, the spirit who now works in the sons of disobedience." The prince is, of course, Satan, who exercises control over this world (1 John 5:19).

Some Christians struggle with the idea of Satan having power, authority, or control over this world. Of course, God is ultimately in control of everything, but He has allowed Satan to exercise a measure of control over this world for the time being. All we have to do is look around at the violence and destruction in the world today to know that Satan is at work. And when we are spiritually dead, without discernment, we are deceived by what Satan does—deceived into walking "according to the course of this world" ourselves.

We Were Disobedient (2:2b)

Every person in the world (including Christians) is disobedient. Hopefully, once we become Christians, we are less disobedient than before. But no one is perfectly obedient toward God. Therefore, no one would ever make it to heaven on their own. No one lives up to God's standards or even to their own standards.

"Sons of disobedience" refers to Satan's family. There are two families in the world: God's and Satan's. Jesus referred to "your father the devil" when addressing the Pharisees (John 8:44), and the apostle John refers to "the children of God and the children of the devil" (1 John 3:10). Some people are offended by the Bible referring to non-Christians as children of the Devil, but that's what the Bible says. It is a serious matter to be separated from God.

We Were Defiled (2:3a)

"Lusts" doesn't refer just to sexuality here; the meaning is much broader. It basically refers to unbridled desires; doing what we want, when, how, and with whom we want; viewing ourselves as the center of the universe. Lusts and desires refers to man living purely for himself and for no one else, a reflection of man's sinful self-centeredness.

What about non-Christian philanthropists? Don't they do good works even though they're not Christians? Some do, yes. But behind the gift lies a motive that cannot be for the honor of God since they don't know God. All actions of non-Christians are self-centered in the final analysis. The Bible says our (self-motivated) righteousness is as "filthy rags" before God (Isaiah 64:6).

We Were Doomed (2:3b)

The fifth description Paul gives is the natural outcome of the first four: We were doomed. He says we were "by nature children of wrath," meaning we were those who justly deserved God's wrath for our sinful disobedience against Him.

Now Paul is preaching this message to Christians in order to remind them of whence they had come. Had it not been for the power of God Paul mentioned in chapter one (verse 19), we would have remained in our trespasses and sins. No Christian can take any personal pride in having somehow solved his sin problem apart from God. Alienated from Him, we were doomed to receive His judgment.

Paul uses two powerful words in verse four which point out just how doomed we were except for the grace of God: "but God." Those two words are, in a manner of speaking, the theme of the whole Bible:

Adam and Eve were lost forever because of their sin, *but God . . .*

Noah would have been drowned with the rest of the people of the world, *but God . . .*

Abraham would have been forever forsaken because of his sin, *but God . . .*

Jonah would never have been given a second chance, *but God . . .*

God always makes the difference in situations where man is hopeless. We were lost in our trespasses and sin, *but God . . .*

THE REMEDY OF SALVATION: PRESENT (2:4-6, 8-9)

Paul now turns to the remedy for our alienation from God, and uses a series of rich terms to describe what God did.

Rich Mercy (2:4a)

Mercy means the withholding of a penalty that was deserved. Whenever I hear someone express a desire for justice, I want to correct them and say, "You don't want justice; you want mercy." Justice means we get what we deserve; mercy means we don't get what we deserve.

Psalm 103:8–12 is a central passage on the mercy of God:

8 The Lord is merciful and gracious,
    Slow to anger, and abounding in mercy.

9 He will not always strive with us,
    Nor will He keep His anger forever.

10 He has not dealt with us according to our sins,
    Nor punished us according to our iniquities.

11 For as the heavens are high above the earth,
    So great is His mercy toward those who fear Him;

12 As far as the east is from the west,
    So far has He removed our transgressions from us.

God is rich in mercy, which is exactly what sinners need. Because God is rich in mercy, there is no sin so deep that God's mercy can't cover it. He has more mercy than we have guilt and shame.

Great Love (2:4b)

God's love for us is great. In fact, it is His great love that motivated Him to pour out His mercy upon us. When we ask, "Why does God love me?" the answer is "Because God is love" (1 John 4:8, 16). God loved the world so much that He gave His only Son that we might have everlasting life by believing in Him (John 3:16). God's loving-kindness in the Old Testament (Hebrew *hesed*) and His love in the New Testament (Greek *agape*) are the focal point of His character (Romans 5:8; 1 John 4:9–10).

Because God is love, He is also rich in mercy. If you were the only human being on the face of the earth, His love would still be directed toward you because that is who He is. It is in His very nature to love and to save.

Rich Grace (2:5b–7, 8)

The third part of God's salvation formula is that He is rich in grace: "by grace you have been saved." Three times in this brief section, Paul mentions God's grace (verses 5, 7, 8).

God's mercy keeps back from us the judgment we deserve. But grace gives to us what we don't deserve. God withholds the penalty of sin then gives us the gift of righteousness in Christ so we can pass the holiness test. The only way we pass the test of God's standard of perfection is to have Christ take the test for us, which He did. And because Christ scored "100," we get that same score because we are in Him.

Grace is **G**od's **R**iches **A**t **C**hrist's **E**xpense. Paul knows all too well of what he speaks when it comes to grace because he knows what he had been: the chief of sinners (1 Timothy 1:13–15). He not only blasphemed Christ, he persecuted the followers of Christ. But God's rich grace saved Him. He got what he didn't deserve, just like you and me.

To the Protestant Reformer John Bradford (d. 1555) is attributed the statement, "There goes John Bradford, but for the grace of God," upon seeing a criminal pass by on the way to execution. And who among us could not say, Amen! to his statement? For it is only the rich grace of God that has reached out and saved any of us from destruction.

Free Gift (2:8–9)

The fourth part of the formula is that salvation is a free gift. That almost goes without saying since mercy, love, and grace are behind it.

Anyone who is a Christian is so because at some point he accepted the free gift of salvation offered by God. That is the only way one enters the kingdom of God: "For by grace you have been saved through faith, and . . . it is the gift of God." Many Westerners have a hard time receiving something that's free because "there's no such thing as a free lunch." It's the American way to earn what you get.

What if, at Christmas, you insisted on paying for the gifts you received? Why, they would no longer be gifts! You might as well have gone to the store and bought them for yourself. A gift is only a gift if you receive it with no cost to you. And that is the good news of the Gospel: salvation is a free gift from God to us.

Through Faith (2:8)

Even if the gift is free, I only get the gift if and when I receive it. If I pay for it, it's not a gift; and if I put off receiving it, it's not a free gift to me. Paul says we have been saved by grace "through faith." And the way we receive the gift of salvation is by reaching out and taking it—by faith.

Faith means, **F**orsaking **A**ll **I** **T**rust **H**im. You receive the gift of salvation by trusting God at His word. You believe that Jesus Christ is your only hope for forgiveness and salvation so you put your trust in Him. You can believe in grace, love, mercy, and the freeness of the gift of salvation—but until you receive it by faith, it is not yours and you are not saved.

THE RESULT OF SALVATION: FUTURE (2:7, 10)

We come now, in conclusion, to the two results of salvation.

For God (2:7)

Simply put, the result of God's saving us is that "in the ages to come He might show the exceeding riches of His grace in His kindness toward us in Christ Jesus." Every Christian is a trophy of God's grace, and heaven is going to be filled with them. God gets an eternity with His redeemed children as a result of saving us.

For Man (2:10)

The result of salvation for us is that we might do the "good works, which God prepared beforehand that we should walk in them." We are not saved *by* good works, but we are most certainly saved *for* good works. What we could not do on our own to earn our salvation, God gives us to do by His grace to demonstrate our salvation.

Throughout the New Testament we are reminded of our responsibility to do those things which are pleasing to God (John 15:8; 2 Corinthians 9:8; 2 Timothy 3:16–17; Titus 2:4; James 2:17. If we become Christians but don't change and do good works, then we haven't really become Christians. Works are not the cause of salvation, but they are an evidence of it. We are God's "workmanship" (Greek *poiema,* from which comes English "poem"), crafted by Him to do His works.

This passage of Ephesians takes us from the lowest point to the highest point in spiritual terms, from being "dead" to being a spiritual "poem" written by God to bring Him glory. And the change has come only as a result of His mercy, love, and grace— the free gift of salvation which has made all the difference.

APPLICATION

1. Read Romans 3:9–18.

   a. Who is Paul describing in these verses? (verse 9)

   b. How many people on their own seek after God? (verses 10–11)

   c. How many people on their own do good for the glory of God? (verse 12)

   d. What do the references to throats, tongues, lips and mouths mean? (verses 13–14)

   e. What else characterizes humanity apart from God? (verses 15–17)

   f. What is the basic cause of mankind's spiritual condition? (verse 18)

2. Read Romans 3:21–24.

    a. What did God reveal in Christ? (verse 21)

    b. How is the righteousness of God obtained? (verse 22)

    c. To whom is it available? (verse 22)

    d. Explain the meaning of verse 23 in terms of missing God's mark, or target, or righteousness.

    e. Compare verse 24 with Ephesians 2:8–9:

3. Read Romans 5:12–21.

    a. How did sin enter the world? Who is the "one man?" (verse 12)

    b. How does verse 12 explain the sinfulness of an "innocent," newborn infant?

    c. What did Adam's sin bring to the human race? (verse 16)

d. What did Christ's gift bring to the human race? (verse 17)

e. Compare/contrast the acts and results of the two individuals, Adam and Christ. (verse 19)

f. When man increases his sin, what does God increase? (verse 20)

g. What was God's purpose and intent in overcoming sin with grace? (verse 21)

4. How did your understanding of your "lostness" change after you became a Christian and understood God's righteousness?

a. How has becoming a Christian changed your view of humanity in light of Ephesians 2:1–3?

b. How and why did you receive the free gift of salvation? Hesitantly? Energetically? Joyfully? Slowly?

c. How do you know that you have indeed received that gift?

5. Record what you learn about the love of God from the following verses:

   a. Jeremiah 31:3

   b. Jonah 4:2

   c. John 3:16

   d. Romans 5:8

   e. 1 John 4:8–10.

6. For what aspect of God's love are you most thankful, and why?

DID YOU KNOW?

The prophet Isaiah offers a stunning picture of the righteousness (or lack thereof) of the natural man in rebellion against God. He says that "we are all like an unclean thing, and all our righteousnesses are like filthy rags" (Isaiah 64:6). The "unclean thing" would be like a person with a terrible disease, considered unclean and an outcast from the community while he was sick (Leviticus 5:2; 13:45). The "filthy rags" referred to are those used by a woman during her monthly cycle; also considered unclean by the Israelites (Leviticus 15:19–24). Uncleanness in Israel was a condition requiring separation from the community and from God until the uncleanness was rectified. The separation Paul describes in Ephesians 2 is the same. Man is "unclean" before God until cleansed of sin by the blood of Jesus Christ.

LESSON **5**

THE BEAUTIFUL BODY OF CHRIST

Ephesians 2:11–18

In this lesson we learn how God has united Jews and Gentiles into one new body, the church.

OUTLINE

All over the world, divisions exist between people: racial, religious, socio-economic, educational, gender, cultural. Satan loves to exaggerate these differences and stir up animosity based on them. In Christ, all differences have been done away; the many have been made one.

I. **What We Once Were**
   A. Segregated Socially
   B. Separated Spiritually
   C. Isolated Nationally
   D. Insulated Culturally
   E. Alienated Personally

II. **What We Now Are**
   A. Once We Were Far Off; Now We Are Near
   B. Once We Were Separated; Now We Are United
   C. Once We Were Two Different Men; Now We Are One Man
   D. Once We Were Excluded; Now We Are Admitted

About thirty years ago, the pastor of a prosperous white church in the southern part of our country became burdened for his community at large. There was an African-American janitor in his church who was a very gracious and obedient Christian, and the pastor and janitor began to have a weekly Bible study and time of prayer together. After a few months of this, the church board found out about it. They approached the pastor and told him that he would have to stop having fellowship with the African-American janitor because it was bad for the church's image.

The pastor told his board he couldn't stop doing that because he felt that fellowshipping with his friend was the Lord's will. And he would not stop, no matter what they said.

Within the next few days, virtually no store in that town would do business with that pastor. He could not buy clothes. He couldn't buy gas or groceries. Before long, he had a nervous breakdown. He was taken to the psychiatric ward in a hospital in a nearby larger city, and on the second day he was there, he dived out of the second story window and committed suicide.

Sin divides our world in so many ways. The true story you've just read is an example of racial and social division in a small southern town. But there is also economic division and religious division among people as well. Sin always divides. It is no accident that one of the main themes in the New Testament is unity within the body of Christ. Unity overcomes the divisions brought about by sin.

It is difficult for us today to imagine the extreme animosity that existed between Jews and Gentiles when Jesus Christ came upon the scene in the first century. Both Jews and Gentiles became His followers—two groups who had never been united over anything previously. In the section of Ephesians 2 we'll study in this lesson (verses 11–18), the apostle Paul goes beyond what God has done for us in Christ individually (2:1–10). He will now show how Christ brings unity in one new body called the church—a group where all prior distinctions of race, gender, religion, and social status are done away with. Ephesians and the book of Acts show how it was God's plan to unite followers of Christ into a glorious, unified body of believers.

Jews believed that Gentiles had been created by God to fuel the fires of hell. They referred to Gentiles as dogs, believing Jews were the only people God loved. Some Jewish women would refuse to help a Gentile woman give birth—if they did, yet another despised Gentile would make its way into the world. You can imagine how the Jews felt when Gentiles began to respond to the Gospel on Paul's missionary journeys. That God would welcome Gentiles into His favor was unthinkable.

We know that it takes time for the sanctification process of God's Spirit to transform our prejudices, biases, and judgments. Who hasn't had that experience even today? That's what was going on in the early years of the Christian church in the first century. And that is what Paul addresses in this section of Ephesians 2. Ephesus was a Gentile city, so Paul directed his comments to the Gentile believers in the church, reminding them of what God had done for them by grafting them into the church with the Jews.

Two key words form a simple outline for this part of Ephesians: "once" in verse 11 and "now" in verse 13. Paul rehearses for the Gentile believers in Ephesus what was "once" true about them and what is "now" true after believing in Christ.

WHAT WE ONCE WERE (2:11-12)

Because the vast majority of the church in America is made up of Gentiles, we can allow Paul's words to the Ephesian Gentiles to describe what we "once" were as well.

Segregated Socially

Paul uses the terms "Uncircumcision" and "Circumcision" to refer to the Gentiles and Jews, respectively. This refers to the rite of covenant confirmation given by God to Abraham (Genesis 17) whereby all Jewish males would be circumcised. This would set them apart from Gentiles who were not normally circumcised (Acts 16:1–3). The Jews took great pride in their circumcision, referring to Gentiles as "the uncircumcised." Circumcision was just one more thing that the Jews had which Gentiles didn't have— and the Jews rubbed it in whenever possible.

A couple of illustrations from the Old Testament point out the use of "uncircumcision" as a derogatory reference toward the Gentiles. When young David went out to fight the Philistine giant, Goliath, David called out, "For who is this uncircumcised Philistine, that he should defy the armies of the living God?" (1 Samuel 17:26). David was saying, "How could this uncircumcised Gentile dog possibly defeat the armies of God?"

Later in the same book, King Saul was severely wounded in a battle with the Philistines. Rather than be found wounded by the

Philistines and killed by them, he called on his armor-bearer to finish him off: "Draw your sword, and thrust me through with it, lest these uncircumcised men come and thrust me through and abuse me" (1 Samuel 31:4). He would rather have been killed by his Jewish armor-bearer than suffer the disgrace of being killed by an uncircumcised Philistine soldier.

Social and cultural separation is not a new phenomenon; it is as old as the human race. Segregation is a result of sin which entered the human race in the Garden of Eden. Israeli and Palestinian hostilities, blacks versus whites, Protestants versus Catholics in Northern Ireland—all are just modern expressions of ancient sins of separation and segregation.

But at the time of the writing of Ephesians, circumcision versus uncircumcision—Jews versus Gentiles—was the flash point. Paul went about teaching the churches that "neither circumcision nor uncircumcision avails anything" (Galatians 5:6).

Separated Spiritually

Not only were Jews and Gentiles segregated socially, they were separated spiritually. That is, the Gentiles had no expectation of a redeemer at all, whereas the Jews had the promise of a coming Messiah. The hope of the advent of the Messiah bound the Jews together during times of oppression; the Messiah was foretold by the Old Testament prophets. But the Gentiles had nothing that came close to the Jews' hope of redemption through an Anointed One who would come to deliver them and elevate them to a new and higher plane of existence. The Gentiles were "without Christ," Paul says.

The Jews were one people, unified by many things spiritually (the Law, circumcision, the temple, the prophetic hope for the future). But Gentiles were divided into numerous nations, all with a distinct pagan perspective on spiritual matters. They had no unified hope, no central spiritual heritage. They had nothing to live for except the here and now. The Jews and Gentiles were totally incompatible spiritually.

Isolated Nationally

Nationally, Gentiles were "aliens from the commonwealth of Israel." Gentiles were outsiders looking in on this unique nation that claimed to be God's chosen people—which the Jews were.

God created Israel through the descendants of Abraham, Isaac, and Jacob to be His chosen race. It was God's intent that Israel should so reflect the glory of God that the nations of the earth would be drawn to God through Israel (Zechariah 8:23). It is utterly amazing that the nation of Israel still exists today, having been reestablished in 1948 in their homeland. And in just the half-century since their rebirth as a national entity, they have occupied center-stage in world affairs.

The Gentiles were a rag-tag collection of small nation-states, warring with each other for power and prominence. But the Jews were a nation envied by the world, especially under the reign of Solomon. The Jews had everything nationally that the Gentiles lacked.

Insulated Culturally

Who were God's covenants with in the Old Testament? Israel, of course. The Mosaic, Abrahamic, and Davidic covenants were all given by God to the Jews. They were promises having to do with the future and destiny of Israel, not the Gentiles. Many children learn in Sunday school the same little chorus I did, part of which says, "Every promise in the book is mine, every chapter, every verse, every line." It wasn't until I was older that I learned that isn't true. I am a Gentile, and the promises of God to Israel in the Old Testament were not given to me. That's why Paul tells the Ephesians they were "strangers from the covenants of promise."

Alienated Personally

As a result of all these separations and isolations, the Gentiles had "no hope and [were] without God in the world." Isn't that a sad statement? All the Gentiles had were their deaf and dumb idols of wood, metal, and stone. They did not know the one true God.

By these hard and somewhat depressing statements, Paul is trying to help the Gentile believers in Ephesus understand their origins, from whence they had come. They had been like a captainless ship adrift on the seas of the world. They could have been described by the inscription above the door to hell in Dante's *Divine Comedy:* "Despair of hope, all ye who enter here." They were without Christ, without citizenship, without covenants, without the Creator, and without Christian hope. They were, and we were, until coming to know Christ.

That's what the "once" refers to in verse 11. How fortunate and blessed are those who are no longer described by Paul's words in verses 11–12. "Now" (verse 13) things are different, and all because we have been brought near to God through Christ.

WHAT WE NOW ARE (2:13-18)

The rest of this section of chapter two focuses on what we are now, what Christ has done for us in making us part of the family of God.

Once We Were Far Off; Now We Are Near (2:13)

As Paul closed with a summary statement in verse 12—"having no hope and without God in the world"—so he opens with one in verse 13: "But now in Christ Jesus you who once were far off have been brought near by the blood of Christ."

The distance-related words ("far off" and "near") are from God's point of view. Gentiles were far away from God, spiritually speaking, but now have been "brought near"—which means "brought to." Every person who is in Christ has been brought to God through the shed blood of Christ—there is no other way (Acts 4:12). Before Christ died for us, we were far off. Now that His sacrifice has been made, and we have embraced it personally, we are near to God.

Once We Were Separated; Now We Are United (2:14)

How did that happen? Paul gives the answer: "For He Himself is our peace, who has made both one, and has broken down the middle wall of separation."

This is an important cultural reference to Jerusalem in the first century. On the periphery of the temple complex in Jerusalem was the court of the Gentiles where they were allowed to gather. They could not enter into the inner court where the Jews were allowed, but at least they could gather on the outside of a barrier set up to separate the Jews from the Gentiles. The Jews tried to proselytize the Gentiles, to make Zionists out of them.

So the Gentiles (as well as Jewish women) were separated from the Jewish men by a wall of separation. But Paul says Jesus broke down the wall of separation between Jews and Gentiles, between men and women. Notice the words "both" and "one." "Both" refers to the two separate groups of Jews and Gentiles; "one" refers to the church of Jesus Christ in which the two have been made one. Through the shed blood of Christ, all the barriers which separate individuals—racial, religious, gender, social, economic—have been torn down. All who believe in Christ have been made one—not only one with God but one with each other (Galatians 3:28).

Once We Were Two Different Men; Now We Are One Man (2:15–16)

The way Christ tore down the wall of separation between Jew and Gentile was by "[abolishing] in His flesh the enmity, that is, the law of commandments contained in ordinances." The ceremonial law code, prescribed in the Mosaic law code, was abolished by Christ's death on the cross. Had it not been, we would still be bringing lambs to church every Sunday to offer as sacrifices for our sin. The ceremonial law which the Jews had, and from which the Gentiles were excluded, was abolished by Christ's death on the cross. Therefore it could no longer be a point of division between Jew and Gentile.

God didn't make Jews become Gentiles or Gentiles become Jews. Rather, He created something new—a new person, called the church. There are no longer Jews and Gentiles, religiously speaking, but only Christians—believers in Christ. That is not to say there are no longer cultural distinctives which characterize the Jewish or Gentile peoples, but they do not separate. What characterizes each group now is their unity and faith in Christ (Romans 10:12; Colossians 3:11; Galatians 3:26 ff.).

Those in Christ are now identified by Him, not by our own individual differences. We aren't known because we are black or white, rich or poor, Gentile or Jew, male or female. All those barriers have been torn down so that now we are known as "Christ-ones"— as Christians. The church is not identified by any label except "Christian" because all of its members, regardless of who they are or where they are from, are one in Christ.

Once We Were Excluded; Now We Are Admitted (2:17–18)

The Gospel was, and is, being preached to all who are far off. People all over the world, Jews and Gentiles, are responding to the Gospel and gaining access to God through the blood of Christ and the power of the Spirit. We gain "access . . . to the Father" not because of our rank or religion or race, but because of Jesus Christ.

The story is told of a young boy standing outside the gates of Buckingham Palace asking to see the king of England. The guards tried to shoo him away until the king's son, the Prince of Wales, appeared and escorted the child into the royal palace, right into the king's own quarters. The boy gained access to the king through another, just as we gain access to God through Christ.

I pray you have gained that access for yourself, that you are able to identify the difference between "once" and "now" in your own life. If you can't, you may still be far off, not yet having drawn near to God through Christ. Today is the day to draw near! The Gospel of peace has been preached to you. I pray you will receive it and begin living with, instead of without, God in this world.

APPLICATION

1. Read James 4:1–3.

   a. What is this passage about?

   b. What does James say is the source of wars and fights among people?

   c. To whom is James writing—Christians or non-Christians? Are Christians immune to divisions which arise because of personal lusts and desires?

   d. Instead of causing divisions and separations among people, what are we supposed to do with our desires and wants? (verses 2b–3)

   e. How could focusing on God instead of on personal differences cause a nation (or the world) to become free of separations and divisions between people?

2. Against what groups of people did you grow up holding prejudices or biases as a young person?

   a. How did you, or your family, exercise those prejudices?

   b. How have those feelings changed since becoming a Christian?

c. Are there any negative sentiments that your children might pick up from you based on your actions today? What steps do you take with your children to teach them not to separate themselves from other people based on external differences?

3. Read Romans 14:1–15:7.

   a. What kind of division had developed in the church at Rome? (verse 14:2)

   b. What principle does Paul communicate concerning this problem? (verses 14:3–4)

   c. What principle is found in verses 14:10–12 concerning judging another?

   d. What should be the focus of the kingdom of God? (verse 14:17)

   e. What do we too often make the focus? (verse 14:17)

   f. Even if you believe you are right in some matter about another person, what should you do with your beliefs? (verse 14:22a)

   g. If you consider yourself right (strong), what is it your responsibility to do? (verses 15:1–2)

h. What example did Christ leave us in this regard? (verse 15:3)

i. What is God's goal for the church? (verse 15:5)

j. How many voices should the world hear when it comes to our speaking for or about God? (verse 15:6)

k. What is the result of our accepting one another? Conversely, what happens when we don't? (verse 15:7)

4. How have you seen divisions and separations hurt the body of Christ today?

a. Do you think Christians of different races worshipping in their own churches is a good or a bad thing? Should Sunday morning be segregated or integrated?

b. Can there be divisions based purely on personal preference (e.g., native language)? How can we express preferences as Christians while still maintaining unity as a body?

5. A number of indications of Gentiles being blessed by God occur in Isaiah. Record what you learn from the following verses:

a. 11:10

b. 42:1, 6

c. 49:6

d. 60:3

e. 66:19

f. How was Christ the fulfillment of those prophecies?
   (Luke 2:25–32)

DID YOU KNOW?

In the Old Testament, Jews were responsible to show kindness to the aliens (Gentiles) in their midst, since they had been aliens who had been treated harshly in Egypt (Deuteronomy 10:19). Gentiles were to be treated fairly, and their sons were even allowed an inheritance of land within the nation (Deuteronomy 24:14–15; Ezekiel 47:22). Israelite men often married Gentile women (e.g., Rahab, Ruth, Bathsheba), though this practice was stopped after the return from exile (Ezra 9:12; 10:2–44). The beginning of Jesus' ministry was directed exclusively to Jews (John 1:11; Matthew 10:5; 15:24), although He gave indication that the kingdom would become open to Gentiles as well (Matthew 15:21–28; Mark 7:24–30; John 4:1–42). Ultimately, when the Jews rejected Jesus as Messiah, Paul, a converted Jew, was sent as an apostle to the Gentiles to open wide the door of salvation to them (Acts 9:15).

THE PRIORITY OF THE CHURCH

Ephesians 2:19–22

In this lesson we learn why the church is so important to God.

OUTLINE

Watching the construction of a building can be spiritually instructive. One crew surveys, measures, and builds the foundation. They leave, and others build the infrastructure. Still others fit out the building for use. So it is with the church, a habitation God is building for Himself.

I. **A New Fellowship: The Picture of Community**

II. **A New Family: The Picture of Unity**

III. **A New Foundation: The Picture of Continuity**
   A. The Formation: The People
   B. The Framework: The Process
   C. The Function: The Purpose

P eople's lives can be chronicled in lots of different ways: geography, events, vocational path, family changes. If I were to map out a history of my own life, I would do it in terms of nine different churches.

My first church was one my father pastored in Toledo, Ohio, where we attended until the seventh grade. It was a humble place in a rough section of town. One of the few things I remember about it was my Sunday school class being in a converted coal bin in the basement that had a bare light bulb hanging from the ceiling. I also remember a faithful man who taught my class, a man who encouraged me to learn the Bible and to love Jesus. The last two years we moved out of that building into a mansion in Toledo that had been vacated, and the church built an auditorium right on the property. That was my first church.

The second church was Emmanuel Baptist Church in Dayton, Ohio, a traditional, brick-and-steeple downtown church. It was an unusual facility with the auditorium on the second floor which made it hard on seniors since there were no elevators. After two years at that church my father was called to be the president of Cedarville College in Cedarville, Ohio, where I experienced the third church in my life.

Cedarville didn't have a church like we would have normally looked for in a town, so my father and some others started a new church. While it was a good church, those years were a low point for me in my church experience because there were so few young people involved, for whatever reason. I recall those years with not as fond memories as I do other churches I have attended, though I know God was active there. I made it through high school and enrolled in Cedarville College and continued attending the same church. As I matured, I began to grow spiritually and develop various ministries.

During my senior year of college, my father came to me one day and asked if I would go to a small church near Columbus, Ohio, and speak in the morning service. No other college faculty or staff was available, so he turned to me. He said I could just give my testimony and deliver a brief message that would be a blessing to the people. I agreed to go.

This church, the fourth in my journey, was different from any other I had attended. It was out in the country with a cemetery next to it. The members were wonderful farming people, as hospitable as could be. So Donna (now my wife) and I drove to the church and

I preached. They took us to lunch, during which one of the men mentioned how we would also be speaking at the evening service, something my father had failed to tell me. Since I had preached everything I knew in the morning service, I just rearranged it and gave it to them again that evening.

It turned out that Donna and I went back to that church week after week, teaching the Word of God, a process which God used dramatically in my life. It was while preaching in a little country church with a cemetery beside it that God impressed upon my heart that He wanted me to be a pastor. That was a fourth, and very important, church in my life.

After graduating from college (and marrying Donna), we left for Dallas, Texas, to attend seminary. The first week I was there, we visited First Baptist Church of Dallas, pastored by Dr. W.A. Criswell. For a young preacher coming from a small country church, this was a country-come-to-town experience! First Baptist was in the heart of downtown Dallas, covered a couple of city blocks, had a bowling alley and a gym, and Sunday school classes in skyscrapers (well, they seemed like skyscrapers to me). Thousands of people attended this church—I had never seen anything like it. It became the fifth church in my spiritual journey, and we attended for nearly two years. It took me that long just to sit on the front row of the balcony every week and soak up what I was seeing. Dr. Criswell had a profound influence on my life, showing that it was possible to combine a scholarly and faithful approach to teaching the Bible with the passion of an evangelist and preacher.

We left First Baptist to find a smaller church where I could have more of an opportunity to develop a ministry. We found it in the sixth church, Northwest Bible Church in Fort Worth, Texas, about 40 miles from where we lived. I became the youth pastor and choir director. Donna and I would drive over and spend the day: Sunday morning service, Sunday school, short nap (we were both working full-time jobs as well as my going to seminary), then choir practice in the afternoon, evening service, then home to Dallas and seminary. We followed that pattern for two years until I graduated from seminary, and we received God's call to the seventh church.

Haddon Heights Baptist Church in the New Jersey town of the same name was my first post-seminary, vocational pastoral assignment: youth pastor and Christian education director. The church had a pastor who was not only a great preacher but a great leader as well. I began studying preaching at that church under his influence, and God began to fan the flames in my own heart. I knew I wanted to preach the Word.

That opportunity came after two years in New Jersey when the eighth church called us to be their pastor. It wasn't exactly a church, I discovered—just seven families who wanted to have a new church in Fort Wayne, Indiana. So in 1969 we started the Blackhawk Baptist Church in four mobile homes shaped like an "L" on five acres of property. One part of the "L" was large enough to seat 125 people. That turned out to be a 12-year adventure for us, during which time we built two auditoriums, began a Christian school, got involved in television, and saw the church grow to 1,500 people.

In 1981, God called me to the ninth and, as far as I know, the last church I will serve on this earth as pastor: Shadow Mountain Community Church in San Diego, California. For more than two decades, we have enjoyed the love and fellowship of God's people and His blessing in abundance.

Nine churches are the backdrop against which my life has been lived. I have recounted that history for only one reason: to explain that I am supremely committed to the church of Jesus Christ. I have been in lots of different kinds of churches: on the East coast, in the Midwest, Southwest, and West coast. Big ones, small ones; city ones, country ones; humble ones, wealthy ones; mature ones, fledgling ones—all different, yet all the same. The local church is where the heart of God beats strongest.

God has started only three institutions: the family in the Garden of Eden, human government after the Flood, and the church at Pentecost following the death, resurrection, and ascension of Jesus Christ. The church is God's way of creating unity in the midst of diversity on planet earth, giving people a new identity, citizenship, and family. God's magnificent idea was to create, not a Jewish church and a Gentile church, but a single, new church that brought both groups together in one new body.

So far in Ephesians 1 and 2, we have studied Paul's record of God's rich blessings on those called in Christ Jesus; how all who are called have been united together, Jew and Gentile, in the church, which is the body of Christ. In the final four verses of chapter two (19–22), Paul provides some summary thoughts about the importance of the church from three perspectives: fellowship, family, and foundation.

A NEW FELLOWSHIP: THE PICTURE OF COMMUNITY (2:19a)

Paul tells the predominantly Gentile church in Ephesus that they are "no longer strangers and foreigners, but fellow citizens. . . ."

That is a picture of community, a place where there are no strangers. Paul is describing to the Ephesians something that would be naturally incomprehensible: Jews and Gentiles being fellow citizens in the same household of faith. Gentiles are no longer on the outside looking in, no longer strangers and foreigners. That is true today as well. All Gentiles—Russian, Chinese, Bolivian, Indian, whoever is not a Jew—have been invited through Christ into the household of faith God began with the father of the Jews, Abraham. The church is made up of all believers everywhere.

Ephesians 3:6 says that Gentiles are "fellow heirs" with the Jews, "partakers of [God's] promise in Christ through the Gospel." So Christ is the door into the new community (John 10:9). When we get to heaven, all the earthly labels come off, and "Child of God through Christ" is the only one that will matter. It wouldn't hurt if we began to live that way on earth as well.

A New Family: The Picture of Unity (2:19b)

The last part of verse 19 says the Gentiles are "fellow citizens with the saints and members of the household of God." The first picture was of fellowship in a new community; this one is of unity in a new family.

Family is a term that suggests warmth and relationships. A family comprises a household, and the Christian family comprises the household of God. Dr. Paul Brand in his book *Fearfully and Wonderfully Made* said this:

> "Just as the complete identity code, the DNA, of my body is found in each individual cell, so also the reality of God permeates every cell in Christ's body, the church, linking us members with a true organic bond. And I sense that bond when I meet strangers in India, Africa, or California who share my loyalty to the Head. Instantly, we become brothers and sisters, fellow cells in Christ's body. I share the ecstasy of community in a universal body that includes every man and woman in whom God resides."

When I leave my personal family at home as I travel, I discover that I never leave the family of God. I meet members of my spiritual family all over the world, brothers and sisters who share my "spiritual DNA" and are, like me, connected by faith to the Head, Jesus Christ. Pilots, flight attendants, hotel employees, taxi drivers, as well as multitudes in churches where I speak . . . all are part of the family of God, the household of faith. There is a tremendous feeling of unity that comes from meeting new family members wherever you go.

A NEW FOUNDATION: THE PICTURE OF CONTINUITY (2:20–22)

Foundations imply stability, steadiness, a confidence of continuity into the future. And that is the third picture Paul gives of the church, the body of Christ. The church could have no firmer foundation—it has been "built on the foundation of the apostles and prophets, Jesus Christ himself being the chief cornerstone."

The Formation: The People

The foundation of the church was formed by people: Jesus Christ, the cornerstone, along with the apostles and prophets.

1. The apostles and prophets

   Jesus promised the apostles that the Holy Spirit would come to teach them and help them remember what He (Jesus) had said (John 14:25–26). What the apostles wrote became the New Testament books, inspired by the Holy Spirit. We don't have prophets and apostles in the church today because, once the foundation was laid, they were no longer needed. In the church, we have moved beyond prophets and apostles to pastors, evangelists, teachers, missionaries, and others— those who are building on the foundation laid by the apostles and prophets.

2. Jesus, the cornerstone

   The cornerstone was the most important piece of the foundation. It was perfectly square so the rest of the foundation, radiating out from it, would be perfectly aligned as well. Because the apostles and prophets built the church off the perfection of Christ, the cornerstone, the foundation they laid was correct. The Old Testament writers foresaw a coming cornerstone (Psalm 118:22; Isaiah 28:16), and Jesus and the apostles identified who it was (Matthew 21:42; Acts 4:11–12). Jesus Christ is the cornerstone.

   If you are going to live in God's house, you have to build on the foundation of the New Testament prophets and apostles whose teachings are aligned perfectly with Jesus Christ, the cornerstone. Any household of faith built on any other foundation is doomed to fall (1 Corinthians 3:11).

The Framework: The Process

Paul's use of a "building" of God, a "holy temple in the Lord," would have evoked images of the temple in Jerusalem for the Jews, perhaps the temple of Diana in Ephesus for the Gentiles. But he is contrasting those structures with the spiritual temple which is the church, a building which is being "fitted together" with all its members, which is you and me and every believer in the world. Each of us has a part to play in the building up of God's spiritual house, the church. God uses us like stones to build up a house in which He can dwell (1 Corinthians 1:10; Ephesians 4:16; Colossians 2:19; 1 Peter 2:5). We are being joined, fitted, or knit together (to use Paul's words) to become the spiritual structure God desires. Christ and the prophets and apostles were the foundation, and we are the framework. When we begin to understand the important part each of us plays in building the church, we will begin to take our role in it much more seriously.

The Function: The Purpose

The purpose of the church is to provide a dwelling place for God on earth. Just as God used to dwell in a temple in Jerusalem made with stones, so He dwells today in a temple made with living stones—believers in Jesus. We, the church, are the temple of God. And when we gather collectively, God dwells in us.

God was in that renovated coal bin with a bare bulb hanging down when I was a child because He dwells in His people. And He was in the church in Cedarville where I struggled during my high school years to find my place. And He has been in all the different churches I've been in since. Not because of me, but because of all the living stones who were faithfully fulfilling their role in building up the temple where He dwells.

If you are a Christian, you are a living stone that God wants to fit together with all the other living stones to build His church. You can't be fit together to form His building if you don't show up. The church is weak today to the extent that living stones are absent and not being fit together.

Think what would happen if no one showed up—then think what would happen if everyone did!

APPLICATION

1. Read Acts 7:44–50, part of Stephen's speech before the ruling Jewish council before he was put to death.

   a. Where did God dwell during the wilderness wanderings? (verse 44)

   b. In order for God to accompany Israel, what did they do with the tabernacle? (verse 45a)

   c. Until the reign of whom did the tabernacle serve as the dwelling of God? (verse 45b)

   d. What request did David make of God? (verse 46)

   e. And who actually built the first permanent temple in Jerusalem as a dwelling place for God? (verse 47)

   f. Since the crucifixion of Christ, where does God *not* dwell any longer? (verse 48)

   g. What inconsistency did Solomon recognize between God and an earthly dwelling even as he was dedicating the temple in Jerusalem? (1 Kings 8:27)

   h. In what two places did Isaiah recognize that God dwelt? (Isaiah 37:16; 40:22)

   i. What do you think Isaiah meant about the dwelling place of God in the passage quoted by Stephen in Acts 7:49–50? (See Isaiah 66:1–2)

   j. If the tabernacle and temple were just temporary symbols of the dwelling of God, what danger might there have been in the Jews exalting the symbol over the reality of God's presence?

k. In Athens, a city rife with temples, why did Paul make the same point to the Greek scholars about God not dwelling in temples made with hands? (Acts 17:24–25).

2. What did God intend to do to establish a spiritual house among Israel? (Isaiah 28:16)

   a. What ultimately happened to the stone He laid? (Psalm 118:22)

   b. Why would builders reject a (literal, not spiritual) cornerstone as unsuitable for the foundation of a building?

   c. Matthew, Mark, and Luke all include Jesus' citation of Psalm 118:22, referring it to Himself; and Peter quotes it twice in Acts and 1 Peter. Why do you think the Jewish builders rejected Jesus as the cornerstone? What were they looking for in a spiritual cornerstone that they didn't see in Him?

3. Read Acts 4:8–13.

   a. Whom did Peter make the focal point of the healing he had performed? (verse 10)

   b. And how did Peter identify Christ? (verse 11)

   c. Given Peter's words in verse 12, what were the ultimate implications for the Jews of rejecting Christ as the spiritual cornerstone of Israel?

   d. The Jews to whom Peter was speaking were Old Testament scholars. What was their reaction to Peter and John's interpretation of the Psalm 118:22 text? (verse 13)

4. Given the importance of the cornerstone, how critical is Jesus to Christianity?

   a. Continuing the analogy, how important would Jesus be as the cornerstone of the spiritual life you are building?

b. Every building takes its orientation from something. What do many people try to use as the cornerstone of a spiritual life besides Christ? What are the results?

c. Complete this sentence: The more intimately I know Christ the cornerstone, the more . . .

5. Read 1 Peter 2:4–8.

a. How does Peter describe Christ? (verse 4)

b. How are we like Christ (Stone vs. stones)? (verse 5)

c. Into what kind of a house are we being built? (verse 5; cf. Romans 12:1)

d. Why do some accept and some reject the cornerstone? (verse 7)

e. What is the core cause of stumbling over Christ? (verse 8)

6. Have you accepted or rejected the cornerstone?

DID YOU KNOW?

The first "building" in which God lived was the Tent of Meeting, or tabernacle, constructed in the wilderness after the Hebrew slaves were led out of captivity by Moses. The tabernacle was to be a place where the glory of God would dwell and be revealed to Israel (Exodus 40:34–35). When Jesus Christ came to earth, the apostle John writes that "the Word became flesh and dwelt among us, and we beheld His glory, the glory as of the only begotten of the Father . . ." (John 1:14). Amazingly, John used a verb, Greek *skenoo*, to describe Jesus dwelling among us. It means "to pitch a tent, or dwell in a tent." Literally, Jesus came and "tabernacled" among His people Israel, but "His own did not receive Him" (John 1:11). God tabernacled on earth in a tent in the Old Testament, and tabernacled in Jesus Christ in the New Testament. Now He dwells in a building not made with hands, the church of those who believe in Jesus.

TWO DIVIDED BY GOD EQUALS ONE

Ephesians 3:1–13

In this lesson we learn even more about why God brought Jews and Gentiles together into one body called the church.

OUTLINE

Have you ever interrupted yourself to provide background information for the benefit of your audience? That's what Paul does in chapter three of Ephesians—digresses to make sure his readers have the background they need to understand the prayer he is about to pray.

I. **The Mystery of the Church**
    A. The Mystery Definitely Revealed
    B. The Mystery Divinely Communicated
    C. The Mystery Dimly Pictured
    D. The Mystery Distinctly Declared

II. **The Minister to the Church**
    A. Appointed
    B. Anointed
    C. Amazed

III. **The Mission of the Church**
    A. To Declare the Truth to Men
    B. To Display the Truth to Angels

IV. **The Ministry of the Church**

One researcher has pointed out that there are more than 33,000 Christian denominations in the world, all of which owe their origin to a church split at some point in their history. Yet it was Jesus Christ who prayed for His followers that they might all live as one (John 17).

The passage we study in this lesson is Paul's reminder to the Ephesians (and to us) about the importance of maintaining unity in the church. This was obviously a timely topic for Paul, as we have already noted, because of the cultural (and other) barriers that existed between Gentiles and Jews who were coming together to form the first churches all over the Mediterranean world.

This passage asks and answers the question, What do you do when you have two cultural groups but there is only one church? Given the number of cultures to which Christianity has spread over the last 2,000 years, and the number of groups into which Christians have divided, this remains an important question for today.

Verses 1–13 are a unique section. Paul begins a prayer in verse 1—then stops and goes in a different direction from verses 2–13, then picks up the prayer again in verse 14. Verses 2–13 are a parenthesis, a digression, in which he adds yet more insight and some new detail to the matters he discussed in chapter two. He wants the Ephesians to know yet again, before he prays for them, how passionately he feels about the subject of unity in the church.

THE MYSTERY OF THE CHURCH (3:1-6)

Paul mentioned the "mystery of [God's] will" in 1:9, but uses it three times (verses 3, 4, 9) with reference to the church.

The Mystery Definitely Revealed (3:1–2)

The mystery of the church is simple: it was an unknown concept in the Old Testament, never even mentioned. It is a new entity made up of Jewish and Gentile believers in Jesus Christ. Some say that Israel was the church in the Old Testament, but that is incorrect. The church was unknown in the Old Testament, which is why Paul calls it a mystery. In fact, the church doesn't begin until Acts 2 when the Holy Spirit is given; and it wasn't explained until Christ commissioned Paul to be the apostle to the Gentiles and explain the concept of the church to Jews and Gentiles alike.

Paul wrote to the Ephesians during his three-year imprisonment in Rome before which he had been imprisoned in Caesarea for two years. Do you know why he had been imprisoned? Ultimately, for preaching the mystery of the church. It started when he was arrested in Jerusalem for preaching the Gospel and allegedly bringing a Gentile (a Greek) onto the temple grounds. This angered the Jewish leaders who nearly started a riot, causing the Romans to arrest Paul (Acts 21:27–29). In verse 1, Paul makes mention of his imprisonment to the Gentiles in Ephesus to remind them that he is in prison for their sake.

The Mystery Divinely Communicated (3:3–4)

The mystery is that the Jews and Gentiles would be unified in one spiritual body—unheard of before now.

How did Paul gain knowledge of the mystery of the church? By divine revelation (verse 3). He didn't read about it in the Old Testament because it's not there. This is a case of "truth being stranger than fiction"—that is, no one, Jew or Gentile, would ever have thought of this. It could have only come from heaven. Perhaps God revealed these truths to Paul shortly after his conversion when he seems to have been out of public view (Acts 9:30; Galatians 1:17). It is clear from Christ's commission to Paul that he was to be an apostle to the Gentiles, which presupposes the revelation of this mystery to him (Acts 9:15–16; 22:21; 26:15–18).

The Mystery Dimly Pictured (3:5)

Paul says that the mystery "in other ages was not made known to the sons of men, *as it has now been revealed* by the Spirit to His holy apostles and prophets" (italics added). Isaiah in particular has a number of references to the Servant of the Lord being a light to the Gentiles (42:6; 49:6), showing that the Gentiles have always been in God's plan of redemption. But no one could have known that the Gentiles would become fellow-heirs of the promises of God with Israel if it had not been revealed "to His holy apostles and prophets." The prophets often wrote things down that they didn't fully understand, and references to Gentile salvation is in that category. So the salvation of the Gentiles was pictured in the Old Testament, but only dimly.

The Mystery Distinctly Declared (3:6)

Max Anders has written a helpful statement on why Paul keeps hammering home this point about the unity of the Jews and Gentiles: "We have trouble understanding why Paul is making such a big deal out of this because we don't understand the degree of separation that existed between the Jews and the Gentiles. It is like saying that there will no longer be blacks and whites in South Africa. It's like saying there will no longer be Catholics and Protestants in [Northern] Ireland. It's like saying there will no longer be liberals and conservatives in the United States. It's like saying all of these people are going to be in one."

To drive the point home again, Paul restates the mystery in three points:

1. The Gentiles are fellow heirs

    Throughout the Old Testament, the Jews lived with the anticipation of being the inheritors of the promises God made to Abraham, Isaac, and Jacob—about the blessings they would experience as God's chosen people. Now, the Gentiles have been made fellow heirs (fellow inheritors). They get the blessings, too—all the same blessings Israel was promised.

2. The Gentiles are fellow members

    Up to the time of Christ and the giving of the Spirit (the birth of the church), to become a child of God, a member of God's household, you had to be or become a Jew. No longer! Now Gentiles could become children of God as well, fellow members "of the same body" (God's family).

3. The Gentiles are fellow partakers

    The Gentiles, according to Paul, are now fellow partakers of the promises in Christ through the Gospel. Everything that is associated with the Gospel of Christ is now not only the full possession of every Jew who believes, but every Gentile who believes as well.

    This was a revolutionary moment in the church and the human race. The Jews, who absolutely despised Gentiles, are now being told that they must move over and allow the Gentiles to become co-participants with them in the blessings of God. We have far too many divisions and separations and tensions in our churches between different groups, especially along racial lines. And this simply should not be. What a testimony we could be to the world of the loving acceptance of God if we would but model the idea of fellow heirs, fellow members, and fellow partakers.

THE MINISTER TO THE CHURCH (3:7–8)

Paul probably could imagine some in Ephesus asking, "Well, who are you to be telling us we are now equal?" So Paul takes a moment to document his role as minister to the Gentiles as appointed by God.

Appointed (3:7)

Paul became the apostle to the Gentiles "by the grace of God." Paul didn't volunteer for the ministry, he was drafted by Almighty God—an experience which marked him and changed him for life. Being in the ministry at the direction of God is the only reason anyone ought ever to be made a minister.

Paul knew about the grace of God; he had been the persecutor of the church in Jerusalem before becoming a Christian. He was actually converted to Christ while on his way to Damascus to throw Christians in jail! He says in 2 Timothy 1:11 that he was "appointed a preacher, an apostle, and a teacher of the Gentiles." And in Colossians 1:25–27 he confirms again his appointment to his ministry to the Gentiles according to a stewardship given him by God.

Paul's credential to be the revealer of the mystery of the church came straight from heaven.

Anointed (3:7b)

Paul not only had the message, he had the power to deliver it. He was not only appointed he was anointed. God's power was at work in Paul to equip him to deliver the message of the mystery of the church all over the Roman Empire. People heard him and responded to the Gospel because of the power of God (the grace of God) at work in and through him.

Paul was the kind of person who was believable because of the power of God at work in him. Paul made an impact for Christ in spite of considering himself the least of the apostles (1 Corinthians 15:9). Yet he was confident of his calling and the grace that was at work in him: "But by the grace of God I am what I am, and His grace toward me was not in vain; but I labored more abundantly than they all, yet not I, but the grace of God which was with me" (1 Corinthians 15:10).

Amazed (3:8)

I don't think Paul ever got over the fact that he was called by God's grace to be a minister of the Gospel. It wasn't false humility on Paul's part. It was just honesty—he couldn't believe God had extended His grace toward him and called him to minister that grace through preaching the Gospel.

You may not think you are worthy to serve the Lord, and that's true—none of us is worthy. But the grace of God can make us worthy in that we are appointed and anointed to do something for Him.

It's amazing that God uses times when we think we've failed miserably to show us His grace was at work. Thirty-three years after I had spoken to a college group early in my ministry (an occasion at which I thought I had completely blown it), a man introduced himself to me and told me he had been in the crowd of college students that night and given his heart to Christ. He had gone on to Bible school and had been in the ministry ever since. Wow! Even when we think we are the chief of failures, God is at work by His grace to do something eternal.

THE MISSION OF THE CHURCH (3:9–13)

Paul completes his parenthetical digression by focusing on the mission of the church—why God has united all believers in one new body by His grace. The mission is to declare the truth of God on earth and in heavenly places.

To Declare the Truth to Men (3:9)

First, the mission is to declare the truth to men: "to make all see what is the fellowship of the mystery, which from the beginning of the ages has been hidden in God who created all things through Jesus Christ."

The church is to be a living testimony of the work of God in man, a place where mercy and grace flow freely for all to see. Instead of acting like we've got it all together, we should acknowledge that we are nothing without the grace of God; that we are just pilgrims on our way, stumbling occasionally as we go, and invite those in the world to join us. How will they believe God can work in their broken lives if they don't see Him working in ours?

The church is to be God's primary visual aid to the world by which they discover that the door to the riches of God's mercy is standing wide open by His grace.

To Display the Truth to Angels (3:10–11)

It is not only men who need to have the wisdom of God preached to them—it is the heavenly hosts as well. The angels of heaven ("principalities and powers") are constantly observing the work of God on planet earth, and Paul says that part of the church's mission is to make God's wisdom known to them. When Gentiles and Jews join together in unity, overcoming barriers that used to divide, I believe the angels must marvel at how the grace of God has brought us together into one new body of believers.

THE MINISTRY OF THE CHURCH (3:12–13)

The ministry of the church in prayer is now one of "boldness and access with confidence through faith in [Christ]." Jews and Gentiles together, as co-heirs of the privileges of God, can enter into the presence of God with confidence. This is in stark contrast to the one day a year when the High Priest, and only the High Priest, could enter the Holy of Holies in the temple to stand in the presence of God. One person, one day per year. Anyone else who went into the Holy of Holies would be struck dead. And if the High Priest did anything wrong while he was in the Lord's presence, he would die as well. (He went in with a cord tied around his ankle so he could be pulled out in case he died.)

But now, anybody who has trusted in Christ, any day of the year, can enter the presence of God boldly and confidently. The writer of the letter to the Hebrews says, "Let us therefore come boldly to the throne of grace, that we may obtain mercy and find grace to help in time of need" (Hebrews 4:16).

To complete this lesson, allow me to pose three questions based on what we've studied in these 13 verses:

1. Do we long for the unity of believers?

    In John 17:21, we have Jesus' request to the Father that His disciples might become one just as Jesus and the Father are one—"that the world may believe that You sent Me." How do you think 33,000 denominations look to the world? Do you think they see us as one?

2. Do we love all the members of God's family?

    Jesus gave us a new commandment that we "love one another" so that all people will know we are His disciples (John 13:34–35). Dorothy Day made this statement: "I really only love God as much as I love the person I love the least." Is there anyone in God's family whom you love less than you should for any reason?

3. Are you looking for ways to reach out to those who might not feel included?

Every Christian who is a member of your church is your brother or sister in the Lord. They are fellow members of Christ's body. Is there anyone in the family who is feeling left out—someone you could put your arms around and make sure they are affirmed in their standing as a fellow member of the body?

How thankful I am for Paul's digression! I trust your appreciation for and understanding of the marvelous mystery of the body of Christ is increasing with each lesson.

APPLICATION

1. Read John 17:9–22.

   a. For whom was Jesus praying? (verse 9)

   b. What request does Jesus make for the disciples three times? (verses 11, 21, 22)

   c. How would unity be an asset in light of circumstances described in verse 14?

   d. What aspect of their mission might lead to splitting apart, or disunity? (verse 18)

   e. How do we know Jesus' prayer was not just for the 12 disciples alone? (verse 20)

   f. What example of unity does Jesus offer as a standard for the disciples' unity? (verses 21–22)

   g. What is dependent on the disciples' oneness and unity? (verse 21b)

   h. What do you think characterizes the oneness of the Father and Son that could also be imitated by the disciples of Jesus in their oneness?

i. What impact do you believe the (dis)unity of the body of Christ has on the watching, unsaved world?

j. Do you believe denominations and other such organizations of Christians are wrong? Are they inherently divisive? Explain your answer.

k. Since most new church structures have formed out of divisive splits, how does that color the current state of Christendom?

l. Are denominations an inevitability in a fallen world? If so, what practical steps could church groups take to promote unity across denominational lines?

2. There are three accounts of the apostle Paul's conversion and commissioning in Acts. Read each and record the common elements you find concerning his calling from God:

a. Acts 9:15

b. Acts 22:21

c. Acts 26:15–18

d. To whom did Jesus Christ specifically send the apostle Paul?

e. How did Paul's background as a persecutor of the church make him an ironic candidate to be an apostle to the Gentiles?

3. Read Acts 15:1–35.

   a. What dispute arose between Jews and Gentiles in Antioch? (verses 1–2)

   b. Where did those come from who brought the teaching that instigated the dispute? (verse 1)

   c. What does this suggest about the thinking in Jerusalem concerning the integration of Gentiles into the church?

   d. What did the leaders from Antioch do? (verse 2)

   e. What good news about Gentiles did they take to the leaders in Jerusalem? And what was the leaders' response? (verses 3–4)

   f. What did some of the believers in Jerusalem, who had been Pharisees (like Paul), say about the Gentiles? (verse 5)

   g. Who took the lead among the Jerusalem leaders in defending the Gentiles? (verses 7–11) But what error had he made before being corrected by Paul? (Galatians 2:11–21)

h. Why was Paul's and Barnabas' testimony so important? (verse 12)

i. What did the council conclude about the Gentiles? (verse 19)

j. How do you explain the requests made of the Gentiles by the leaders in Jerusalem? (verses 20–21)

k. How does this passage of Scripture help you better understand the complexity and difficulty of reconciling a Jewish-Gentile church in the early years of the church?

4. If Paul, the "chief of sinners," was given grace by God, how does that encourage you concerning your own life and ministry?

DID YOU KNOW?

The apostle Paul was imprisoned three times that we know of for the sake of the Gospel. However, those imprisonments began in A.D. 57, and in the letter of 2 Corinthians, written in A.D. 55, he mentions "imprisonments" (6:5) he endured. So it seems likely that he was jailed previous to the three times specifically recorded in the New Testament. Paul journeyed to Jerusalem with the financial collection for the suffering church where he was arrested by the Romans at the behest of Jewish leaders. He was imprisoned at Caesarea for about two years (A.D. 57–59), then taken by ship to Rome where he was under house arrest for two or three years. He was set free, then rearrested in A.D. 67 in Rome where he was martyred for his faith in A.D. 68.

A PRAYER FOR INNER STRENGTH

Ephesians 3:14–21

In this lesson we learn what Paul prayed for the believers in Ephesus.

OUTLINE

Sometimes we're not sure how to pray for a friend or even how to pray for ourselves. Paul's prayer for the Ephesians is a beautiful model of a prayer for strength in the inner man. And who is there who wouldn't benefit from such a prayer for power in the inner man?

I. **The Posture for This Prayer**

II. **The Petitions of This Prayer**
   A. A Prayer for an Inward Power
   B. A Prayer for an Inward Presence
   C. A Prayer for an Inward Perception
   D. A Prayer for an Inward Provision

III. **The Potential of This Prayer**

In the first lesson in our study of Ephesians, I mentioned the importance of inner strength. Our culture conditions us to focus on the outward person in order to meet the expectations of society and other people. But the inner man is the most important, for from the inner person comes the strength to meet the challenges of life. Most Christians can give a testimony to having been carried through a serious test by the inner strength which only the Holy Spirit can provide.

But inner strength doesn't just happen. It is developed and nurtured over time as a result of the intake of truth—and prayer. And in this lesson of our study, we get to listen in as Paul prays for the inner strength of the Ephesian Christians. It becomes a model prayer for us to pray for our own inner strength. I believe Paul's prayer in 3:14–21 is, next to the Lord's Prayer, the most beautiful prayer in the New Testament.

Paul said in 2 Corinthians 4:16 that the outer man is perishing though the inner man is being renewed day by day. Anyone who wants to make it through the trials of this life must learn to develop inner strength. We bow before the Father of the Lord Jesus Christ (verse 14) asking for strength through the Spirit (verse 16). All the members of the Godhead are involved in building up our inner man. That's how important it is.

THE POSTURE FOR THIS PRAYER (3:14–15)

It might not seem noteworthy that Paul says, "I bow my knees to the Father" in prayer. However, it was not common for Jews to pray on bended knee—they usually stood upright (Luke 18:11, 13). (If you see a picture of Jewish men praying at the Western Wall in Jerusalem today, you will note that they pray standing.)

Kneeling is a picture and reminder of Paul's intensity in this prayer. This is not a normal, stand-up prayer; it is an intense, kneel-down prayer. It reminds us of Jesus' posture in prayer on the night He was betrayed: ". . . and He knelt down and prayed" (Luke 22:41). Stephen also knelt down to pray as he was stoned to death (Acts 7:60). Peter knelt down to pray when he prayed for the resuscitation of Dorcas (Acts 9:40). Paul knelt down to pray in his emotional departure from the Ephesian church (Acts 20:36). And the day is coming when every knee shall bow at the appearance of Jesus at His second coming (Romans 14:11; Philippians 2:10).

Kneeling, both outwardly and inwardly, is a symbol of submission. Kneeling says, "You are greater than I am." It is an act of honor or reverence, as in bowing in the presence of a king. And prayer is certainly an appropriate setting for all of these attitudes on the part of the believer. Prayer is a declaration of dependence, not independence. It is our way of telling God that we are dependent on Him for whatever the situation may require.

While in seminary, we attended First Baptist Church in Dallas, where I was surprised to discover that every pew had a kneeling bench. This was unusual for a Baptist church, but it was a powerful experience weekly to get on our knees, along with thousands of others, to pray before God. In addition, the pastor, Dr. Criswell, and his staff on the platform, would kneel as well. There is something special about prayer conducted on bended knee, especially an entire congregation at once.

THE PETITIONS OF THIS PRAYER (3:16–19)

Paul makes four petitions on behalf of the Ephesian believers:

A Prayer for an Inward Power (3:16)

Notice the word "that." Paul says, much as we do today, "Lord, I pray that . . ." "That" introduces a purpose clause: "Here is the purpose of my prayer." And the first purpose is that the Ephesians would be "strengthened with might through His Spirit in the inner man."

Christians don't get a free pass in life when it comes to trouble. We sing of being "safe and secure from all alarms," but that is not our reality. Sometimes we walk straight into the alarms, and for those times we need inner strength. The secret is to cultivate (pray for) inner strength before the alarm bell sounds.

True strength with might comes only from the Spirit. Jesus told the disciples, "For without Me you can do nothing" (John 15:5). If we don't have a strong relationship with Christ through the Spirit before the trials start, it will be difficult to make it through. Note the passage of time implied in both John the Baptist and Jesus as they "became strong in spirit" (Luke 1:80; 2:40). Just as our bodies take time to grow strong, so do our spirits.

A tragedy befell one of our church families recently, and as I prayed in the hospital with one who was involved, her words reflected strength of spirit: "I just want you to know one thing, Pastor. My life is for God. Whatever happens, my life is for God." No one makes that up on the day tragedy occurs. Those words

came from time, prayer, and internalizing the Word of God—
feeding the spirit a diet of godliness so that it will be strong in the
day of trouble.

A Prayer for an Inward Presence (3:17a)

The second purpose ("that") for Paul's prayer is for the inward
presence of Christ. Why does he pray this if Christ is already in the
heart of every true believer?

The answer has to do with the meaning of "dwell in your heart."
That phrase in the Greek language means to settle down and be
at home, not to be just a casual resident. It's the difference in your
being in a house and being *at home* in a house. Often when I travel,
generous and hospitable friends will insist I stay in their home,
which I am often happy to do. But I confess I am so afraid I will
break something or upset their routine or make noise too late at
night—I'm in their home but not *at home* in their home. We're only
at home in our own permanent house. That's what Paul is praying
for the Ephesians, that Christ would feel completely at home in
their hearts.

Robert Boyd Munger's classic booklet, *My Heart, Christ's Home*,
illustrates what it takes to allow Christ to take up residence and
be at home in our hearts. He pictures the heart as a home, and the
different rooms as the different areas of life where Christ wants
to be Lord. As Christ is shown around His new home, He keeps
finding areas of the heart not yet made pure—things on shelves
and in closets that need to be cleaned up and thrown out. And so it
is with our lives. For Christ to dwell in our hearts we have to give
Christ the deed to the whole house; let Him be Lord of everything.
And that is what Paul prayed for the Ephesians.

When Christ is at home in our heart, many of the questions
we ask about what is appropriate and what isn't will be answered.
Just ask, "Would Christ be comfortable with this video, this TV
show, this music?" Learning to think in terms of Christ dwelling
in our heart adds a new dimension to daily guidance.

A Prayer for an Inward Perception (3:17b–19a)

The third purpose ("that") is that the Ephesians (and we) "may
be able to comprehend with all the saints what is the width and
length and depth and height" of the love of Christ. A knowledge of
the love of God in Christ is Paul's third goal for the Ephesian believers.

He prays in four dimensions when praying about the love of
God: width, length, depth, and height. It's hard to know why Paul

used these geometric terms to describe the love of God. But these terms provide good pictures by which to imagine the greatness of God's love.

1. The breadth of His love

   Breadth reminds us that God's love reaches around the world. Missionary outreach programs are a response to the breadth of His love.

2. The length of His love

   Length reminds us that God's love existed before the foundation of the world and reaches into eternity future. There is no beginning and no end to the love of God.

3. The depth of His love

   Depth reminds us that God's love extends to the depths of the human heart. There is no heart where the darkness of human sin is unreachable by the light of God's love. The psalmist says God "brought me up out of a horrible pit . . . and set my feet upon a rock" (Psalm 40:2).

4. The height of His love

   Height reminds us that His love lifts us up to the very throne of God itself where we may enter with boldness to find grace and help in time of need (Hebrews 4:16).

After the Spanish inquisition, it is said that the bones of a Spanish prisoner were found in a dungeon with shackles still attached to his leg bones. Above where the skeleton lay, the prisoner had scratched a cross into the face of the stone wall. At the top of the cross was the word "height," at the bottom the word "depth," at the end of one arm of the cross was the word "breadth," and at the end of the other arm of the cross was the word "length." That Spanish believer had died contemplating "the love of Christ which passes knowledge." The cross is a perfect symbol of the extent of God's love for us.

Love that passes knowledge is almost an oxymoron: how can we know something that surpasses our understanding? The point is that we can't know this love by human knowledge; it is only made known to us through the Holy Spirit being shed abroad in our heart. Only the love of God could cause Jews and Gentiles to have love for one another or cause us to forgive someone who has hurt us. That kind of love surpasses human understanding.

A Prayer for an Inward Provision (3:19b)

The final "that" in Paul's prayer is that the Ephesians would be "filled with all the fullness of God." Notice the progression of these petitions. The inner strength of the Holy Spirit leads us to the indwelling of Christ. The indwelling of Christ leads us to the knowledge of His abundant love. And His abundant love leads us to a fullness of God's presence in us.

In Ephesians 5:18, which we'll discuss in depth when we get there in our study, Paul instructs the Ephesians to be "filled with the Spirit." The Greek word for "filled" doesn't mean filled up like we would a glass of water—up to a certain level. Rather, it means to be controlled by. Therefore, if we are filled with the fullness of God, we will be controlled by God. And to be filled by God, we have to be empty of self. God can't and won't force Himself into a place that is already filled. That requires we empty ourselves of everything so He can fill and control us.

I don't know if any of us have ever emptied ourselves of every single thing that is of our carnal, human nature. But I do know that to the degree I'm aware of God's fullness in my life, that's the best part of me there is. Every time I've tried to do things on my own, and fallen on my face, I've immediately given those things over to the Lord. So it's a gradual process of giving Him more and more control over our lives.

I read a true story, a kind of modern-day prodigal son story, of a young man who lived on the streets as a bum, begging money for a living. One day he touched a man on the shoulder to ask for money, and when the man turned around it was the young man's father. They had a tearful reunion with the father telling his son how everything he had was his. He didn't need to beg for a dime when everything was already his if he would only accept what the father had to give him.

Sometimes we act like that—begging God for a dime here and a quarter there, when He has already given us all the riches of heaven if we would just allow Him to fill us with His fullness. If we would just pray the prayer Paul prayed for the Ephesians and ask God to fill us with His fullness—to make our heart His home.

THE POTENTIAL OF THIS PRAYER (3:20–21)

When we pray like Paul prayed, what can we expect God to do? The same thing Paul promised He would do for the Ephesians: ". . . exceedingly abundantly above all that we ask or think, according to the power that works in us."

If you don't have "who is able" underlined in your Bible, I encourage you to do so. He is able . . . to strengthen the inner man, make your heart His home, give you understanding of His love, and fill you with His fullness. He is able!

I have read this verse out loud with our church on occasion this way, to highlight every single thing God is able to do:

He is able to do

He is able to do exceedingly

He is able to do exceedingly abundantly

He is able to do exceedingly abundantly above

He is able to do exceedingly abundantly above all

He is able to do exceedingly abundantly above all that we ask

He is able to do exceedingly abundantly above all that we ask or even think.

I can't think of a better way to conclude this lesson than to read Paul's prayer for the Ephesians from Eugene Peterson's Bible translation, *The Message:*

"My response is to get down on my knees before the Father, this magnificent Father who parcels out all heaven and earth. I ask him to strengthen you by his Spirit—not a brute strength but a glorious inner strength—that Christ will live in you as you open the door and invite him in. And I ask him that with both feet planted firmly on love, you'll be able to take in with all Christians the extravagant dimensions of Christ's love. Reach out and experience the breadth! Test its length! Plumb the depths! Rise to the heights! Live full lives, full in the fullness of God. God can do anything, you know—far more than you could ever imagine or guess or request in your wildest dreams! He does it not by pushing us around but by working within us, his Spirit deeply and gently within us.

"Glory to God in the church!
Glory to God in the Messiah, in Jesus!
Glory down all the generations!
Glory through all millennia! Oh, yes!"
(Ephesians 3:4–21)

APPLICATION

1. The words "strong," strength," and "strengthen" occur 432 times in English from Genesis through John (*NKJV*), but only 30 times from Acts through Revelation. What do you make of those lopsided numbers?

   Describe the kind of strength referred to in each of these New Testament verses.

   a. Acts 9:22

   b. Romans 5:6

   c. Romans 15:1

   d. 1 Corinthians 15:56

   e. 1 Corinthians 16:13

   f. 2 Corinthians 12:9

g. 2 Corinthians 12:10

h. Hebrews 11:34

i. Hebrews 12:12

j. 1 John 2:14

k. Revelation 3:2

l. Revelation 3:8

m. How would you summarize the predominant emphasis of these verses?

n. In the broadest of terms, the Old Testament is more about

_____ strength while the New Testament is more

about _____ strength. (physical, spiritual)

2. Read Matthew 7:24–27.

   a. To whom does Jesus address verses 24–25?

   b. To whom are verses 26–27 addressed?

   c. Why might the word "strength" qualify as the topic of both these short parables?

   d. How is the presence of strength illustrated in verses 24–25?

   e. How is the absence illustrated in verses 26–27?

f. Are these two parables about structural construction techniques? If not, what is the meaning in real-life terms?

g. To which of His specific teachings was Jesus referring? What phrase does Matthew 13:19 contain that might be a summary description of all His teachings?

h. Based on the way you handle adversity in your life (either overall or recently), which person are you most like of the two described in the parables?

3. From your general knowledge of Jesus' teachings (or New Testament teachings in general), list three truths about God that give you the most inner strength in times of adversity.

a.

b.

c.

d. In terms of hours each week, compare the time you invest in maintaining or increasing your physical strength versus maintaining or increasing your spiritual strength.

e. How would you compare the importance or priority of these two areas of life?

f. In what ways can physical strength or health (or the lack of it) impact spiritual strength or health?

g. What adjustments might be called for in either category of your life?

DID YOU KNOW?

Scripture records examples of various postures for prayer. Most common was standing (1 Kings 8:22; Nehemiah 9:4–5). People also sat (1 Chronicles 17:16; Luke 10:13), knelt (Ezra 9:5; Acts 20:36), bowed down (Exodus 34:8), laid prostrate on the ground (2 Samuel 12:16; Matthew 26:39), and lifted up holy hands (Psalm 28:2; 1 Timothy 2:8). People prayed alone, silently (1 Samuel 1:12–13), alone, aloud (Ezekiel 11:13), in groups of two or three (Matthew 18:19), and in large groups (Psalm 35:18). Prayer was offered in the morning (Psalm 5:1–3), evening (Genesis 24:63), at fixed times (Psalm 55:17), and at all times (Romans 1:9).

WALKING IN UNITY

Ephesians 4:1–6

In this lesson we learn what we have to believe and how we have to behave to preserve unity in the church.

OUTLINE

In spite of all the denominations and groups in Christendom, it is possible for the church of Jesus Christ to be united without being part of an ecumenical movement. We have to share core beliefs which are central to the faith and core values which allow imperfect people to live together.

I. **The Plea for Unity in the Church**
   A. Purpose
   B. Progress
   C. Perseverance

II. **The Points of Unity in the Church**
   A. One Body
   B. One Spirit
   C. One Hope
   D. One Lord
   E. One Faith
   F. One Baptism
   G. One God

III. **The Practice of Unity in the Church**
   A. Humility
   B. Meekness
   C. Patience
   D. Forbearance

IV. **The Price of Unity in the Church**

W
hile preaching through the book of Ephesians in my church, I asked our congregation to do a strange thing. I asked them, on the count of three, to shout out the name of their church background, whatever it might be—Baptist, Pentecostal, Methodist, Catholic, Charismatic, Presbyterian, whatever. I counted to three and . . . it was amazing! I could barely pick out the word "Baptist" out of the cacophony of sound that roared forth (most of our folks have a Baptist background). I suppose we have members and regular attendees from almost every church background in the United States.

The purpose of that exercise was to illustrate to the congregation just how diverse the body of Christ is. Yet, above that diversity, reigns that which is a priority in the heart of God: the unity of believers. Sadly, all of Christendom is not as unified as the members in a given local church, but it is God's will that we be so unified. And that is on the apostle Paul's heart as he writes to the church in Ephesus—especially in chapter four, which we begin with this lesson.

The first three chapters of Ephesians detail what God has done for us in Christ. We've "counted our blessings" as the recipients of God's infinite riches in the Savior. But beginning with chapter four, Paul switches from doctrine to duty; he turns the spotlight on our application of the truths he has set forth in the first three chapters.

I find it significant that, as Paul turns to the application of truth, he doesn't talk about evangelism, prayer, or worship. First on his list is unity within the church, the topic of Jesus' prayer to the Father in John 17.

In this lesson we will look at the first six verses of Ephesians 4: the plea, points, practice, and price of unity in the church.

THE PLEA FOR UNITY IN THE CHURCH (4:1)

Ephesians was written during Paul's first of two imprisonments in Rome, as evidenced by him calling himself "the prisoner of the Lord." He was not the prisoner of emperor Nero or the Roman Empire, but of Christ. It was God's purposes that caused him to be in jail.

Paul's plea is that the Ephesians "walk worthy of the calling with which [they] were called." And what was their (our) calling?

Simply put, our calling is to be children of God. In Philippians 3:14 the calling is an "upward" calling, and in 2 Timothy 1:9 it is a "holy" calling. First Corinthians 1:26 says we have a humble calling, and Hebrews 3:1 caps all the descriptions saying it is a "heavenly" calling. And Paul says our walk should match the nobility and nature of our calling.

I remember when, as a child, I would get ready to go to camp and my mother would sit me down and tell me to remember who I was while I was away. I was never sure what that meant, except that I was a preacher's kid and I'd better behave! She probably had in mind something like Paul said here, that I needed to walk worthy of my calling as a Christian.

The word "worthy" is interesting—it has reference to a balance scale. It's as if we have all that God has done for us on one side of the scale, and our life on the other side should balance that out. Not in the sense of earning or paying for what God has done but in terms of our recognition of what God has done for us, our lives should reflect a proper understanding of what God has done for us. I believe the walk of most Christians doesn't reflect a proper understanding of what God has done for them. Our lives are out of balance, out of sync, with what God has done. To gain an understanding of "walking worthy" would be to change the life of the average Christian.

Because I grew up in Ohio, I'm naturally a fan of the Ohio State Buckeyes football team. When they played for the national championship title in 2002, most people expected them not to win. But they did! And after I read a copy of the speech the coach delivered to the players before the game, I wasn't surprised. He reviewed for the players the great history and tradition of Ohio State University football. He talked about the legendary coach Woody Hayes, about the ivy covered walls, the fantastic marching band and their famous "Script Ohio" halftime routine. And at the end, he told them (I'm paraphrasing), "I want you to go out there tonight and play in such a way that when you come back to this university in the future, or gather for a reunion 50 years from now, you'll look back on this night and say, 'This was the greatest night in my life!'"

That coach wanted his players to play worthy of their great university—and they did. And that's what Paul is telling us. How much more reason do we have to "play a great game," based on our calling from God, than any football team does?

There are three things to remember as we walk worthily.

Purpose

When we walk, we must walk purposefully. Ours is not a random walk, bouncing through life from pillar to post. It is a purposeful walk according to the calling of God for our life.

Progress

Our walk is to be a measured walk, a walk where progress is evident. If we are not making progress in sanctification—becoming more like Christ—we are not walking worthy of our calling.

Perseverance

We are not to walk and then quit before arriving at our destination. We have no guarantee that our walk will be an easy one, so perseverance is a requirement.

THE POINTS OF UNITY IN THE CHURCH (4:4–6)

There are seven dynamics in the Christian experience which are singular; and because they are singular, they are emblematic of unity. There is not a different kind of baptism for every individual Christian, for example. There is only one baptism, and all believers are to be identified by it. If every Christian identifies with all seven of these points, then all Christians should be unified as one.

One Body

The body of Christ is made up of every single person who has ever accepted Christ at any time in history. Every true Christian is a part of the same body; there is only one. The thousands of different Christian denominations are not thousands of bodies of Christ. We ought to live as if we are members of the same family because we are.

One Spirit

There is only one Holy Spirit. There isn't a Charismatic Holy Spirit and a Baptist Holy Spirit, one for America and one for Africa. There is only one Spirit that indwells every Christian in the world. If we are divided on doctrine or practice or any other matter, it is not from the Spirit since the same Spirit indwells us all.

One Hope

With all the different views on the end-time in the Christian church, it seems hard to think that there could be only one hope.

Many Christians find it hard to understand, if there is only one Spirit teaching the church, why there are so many views on prophecy and the end of the age. We should never let these differences in views divide us. I hold my personal convictions on these matters strongly, but I will maintain unity at all costs with others who don't share my views.

The main thing to remember about "one hope" is that Christ is our hope, not our theological viewpoint (Colossians 1:27; Titus 2:13). As long as we stay focused on Him as our hope, we will remain united.

One Lord

In the middle of the seven points is Christ the Lord. It is interesting to note that Christians were not persecuted by the Romans for believing in the Christian God. Nobody was more tolerant of religions than the Romans were. In fact, they had a temple in Rome called the Pantheon dedicated to "all gods." No, it wasn't that the Christians had their own God that caused them to be persecuted. It was because they believed He was the only God, above all the gods with a little "g." There was only one Lord to them, and it wasn't Caesar or any other religion's god. The Bible is expressly clear on the point that Jesus Christ is the only Son of God, the only bridge between God and man (John 14:6; Acts 4:12; 1 Timothy 2:5).

One Faith

This isn't talking about personal faith, it's talking about a system of belief, a body of truth. The beliefs we hold to comprise the faith "once for all delivered to the saints" (Jude 3). Our faith is found in the Bible, God's Word, which is the final authority for all matters of Christian faith and practice. The fact that different groups believe different things about the same verse is due to our imperfections as interpreters. The fact remains there is only one faith. We are not free to make up something different from what the Bible teaches and call it Christianity.

One Baptism

There are several different baptismal practices in the church. Some sprinkle, some immerse; some baptize people of any age, some only adults; and some baptize three times, once each in the names of the Father, Son, and Holy Spirit. Contrary to the way it appears in the church, there really is only one baptism. In the early church, there was a higher price attached to baptism than today, for it was often done in the presence of the community with nonbelievers looking on. It took a serious step of faith to make a public declaration of one's beliefs. And that step was baptism, a singular ordinance whereby entrance into the body of Christ was declared to all.

One God

Monotheism (one God) was at the core of Jewish faith and ultimately Christian faith: "Hear, O Israel: The Lord our God, the Lord is one!" (Deuteronomy 6:4) It is not true that all religions worship one God since all religions do not worship the God of the Bible who is the Father of our Lord Jesus Christ. Unity in the church is centered on the identity of this one God.

To summarize, Paul is not saying there has to be unity in Christendom on the shape of church buildings, the color of the pews, or the kinds of worship songs we sing. Yet sadly, those things often divide us in the body of Christ. Our unity is to be in the seven points he enumerates in verses 5–6. In everything else there is freedom to disagree. As St. Augustine said 1,500 years ago, "In essentials unity, in non-essentials liberty, in all things charity."

THE PRACTICE OF UNITY IN THE CHURCH (4:2)

We turn back to verse two to talk about the practices that will ensure unity on these seven points. I find as I travel around the body of Christ that the lack of unity in churches is caused less often over doctrinal issues (the seven points we just covered) than it is over an inability of people to get along in Christian love. It is God's job to establish the boundaries for unity and our job to preserve the unity through right beliefs and behavior. The practice of four values or attitudes in the church will preserve the unity God has established.

Humility

What Paul calls lowliness, we may refer to as humility. Pride and arrogance, especially on the part of leaders, is the first step toward the loss of unity. No one is any better than anyone else in the church, and that goes for pastors especially. We may stand on a platform because it's better for visibility, but it's certainly not because we are to be lifted up above any other. Every Christian is to have the same attitude in ourselves that Christ Jesus had in Himself when He humbled Himself and became a man on planet earth in submission to the Father's will (Philippians 2:5–8).

Meekness

From humility comes a spirit of meekness (or gentleness). Humble people are gentle people, but they aren't weak people. Meek is not a synonym for weak. Moses, the Bible says, was the meekest man on earth, and he was certainly not weak (Numbers 12:3). Neither was Jesus weak, though He was meek (Matthew 11:29). Meekness is important in preserving unity because it is power under control, or self-controlled strength. When Jesus was being arrested and tried, He could have called legions of angels to come to His aid, but He didn't. And when David was being pursued by Saul in the wilderness, he could easily have taken Saul's life in the cave at Engedi, but he didn't. Both were meek because they exercised control over their power. When one is in the right in the local church, power is not to be used impulsively thereby destroying unity.

Patience

Longsuffering means patience. It comes from the Greek word *macrothumias,* or long temper. If you don't know what long temper means, think about short temper—it's the opposite. If unity is to be preserved in the church, humility will lead to meekness; and meekness will lead to patience—a temper that is long.

Forbearance

Finally, forbearance—my favorite of all four words. The best definition of forbearance I have ever found is this: to put up with someone. Putting up with other people is only possible if we are humble (we think more of them than of ourselves), meek (we are under control), and patient (we don't have a short temper). This side of heaven, all of us are called on to put up with one another. The moment we stop doing that is the moment we lose unity in the church.

We can have unity in the church if we hold Paul's seven-fold doctrinal statement and we do it with humility, gentleness, patience, and forbearance. We come from such a multitude of different backgrounds that we will never be unified in the flesh. It will take the work of the Spirit to give us grace to believe and behave in a unified way.

THE PRICE OF UNITY IN THE CHURCH (4:3)

We must endeavor to keep unity in the body. That means it doesn't come easily, that it's going to be hard work. That is the price of unity—wanting it so badly, in order to walk worthy of our calling, that we're willing to work hard at maintaining it.

Unity doesn't mean uniformity. It doesn't mean we have to all be cookie-cutter Christians. Nor does it mean unanimity—we don't have to agree on everything. Nor is unity an ecumenical movement where we set aside core beliefs to find the lowest common denominator of agreement. Unity is embracing Jesus Christ as Lord of life and Lord of the church, and bowing before Him in all things.

When we concentrate on Who we know instead of what we know, we'll remain united.

1. Read Colossians 1:9–12.

   a. In this prayer of Paul for the Colossians, to what does "for this reason" refer? What is the "reason" he is praying? (verse 9; see also verse 4)

   b. In verses 9 and 10, there are two "that's"—indicating the intended goal or result of Paul's prayer. Identify what these two "that's" refer to.

      • verse 9

      • verse 10

   c. In your opinion, do these two represent separate and equal requests ("that you may be filled" and "that you may walk worthy"), OR, is the first "that" a condition for the "second?" ("that you may be filled" SO THAT "you may walk worthy") Explain your answer:

   d. How does Paul's prayer in verse 9 parallel the exhortation in Proverbs 2:1–7?

   e. How many people do you know whom you think of as having "all wisdom and spiritual understanding?" What do you think this means, practically speaking?

f. Identify five or six aspects of walking worthy of the Lord from verses 10–12:

1.

2.

3.

4.

5.

6.

g. What reasons does Paul cite for "giving thanks to the Father" in verses 13–14?

2. What do you learn about Christian hope from the following verses:

a. Acts 24:15

b. Acts 28:20 (who was the "hope of Israel" for whom Paul was in jail?)

c. Romans 5:4–5

d. Romans 8:24–25

e. Romans 15:4

f. Romans 15:13

g. 1 Corinthians 15:19

h. Galatians 5:5

i. 1 Thessalonians 2:19

j. 1 Timothy 1:1

k. Hebrews 6:19

l. 1 Peter 1:21

m. 1 John 3:33

3. What is the difference between faith and hope?

4. What answer would you give to a critic who called your Christian hope nothing but "pie in the sky, by and by?"

   a. What does the Resurrection add to the discussion of hope? (1 Corinthians 15:13–14)

   b. How is your hope in the promises of God refined and made stronger by trials?

   c. What would you tell a "hopeless" friend about how to gain hope in this world?

5. What do the following verses say about the reality of one way to be saved?

   a. John 14:6

   b. Acts 4:12

   c. 1 Timothy 2:5

DID YOU KNOW?

Some scholars believe that the unique confession found in Ephesians 4:4–6 may represent an early confession, or creed, in use in first-century churches, written either by Paul or someone else. Creeds in their earliest forms were used as confessions of faith at the time of baptism, where the candidate publicly confessed his belief in Christ (see Romans 10:9; 1 Corinthians 12:3). In time, creeds were made longer and incorporated into worship and instruction. The two most famous creeds still in use in the church today are the Apostles Creed, dating from at least the fourth century, used by churches in the West, and the Nicene Creed, used by churches in the East from the time of the Council of Nicea in A.D. 325.

THE GIFT OF A LIFETIME

Ephesians 4:7–12

In this lesson we learn how God has given gifts to believers which we give back to Him in service.

OUTLINE

How would you feel if you sacrificed to get a loved one a gift, but it went unappreciated and unused by the recipient? God's spiritual gifts to the church have suffered a similar fate. Every believer has been given at least one gift, but many have never unwrapped it and put it to good use.

I. **The Provision of Gifts to Individual Believers**
   A. The Gifts of God's Grace
   B. The Grace of God's Gifts

II. **The Price of Gifts for Individual Believers**
   A. The Old Testament Promise
   B. The New Testament Proof

III. **The Purpose of Gifts to Individual Believers**
   A. Gifts for the Foundation of the Church
   B. Gifts for the Formation of the Church
   C. Gifts for the Function of the Church

Has anything suffered as much at the hands of Christmas pundits as the poor fruitcake? Granted, fruitcakes are a long-standing Christmas tradition, and I'm sure they have a noble heritage that goes back to merry old England or some other legendary location. But people still seem to make fun of fruitcakes more than anything else at Christmas. In fact, "fruitcake" has become a playful, if not derogatory, label that we apply to our friends who are, well, a little "nutty." You know what I mean. As part of a Christmas production one year in our church, we did a spoof on fruitcakes. I still have one that has been sent as a joke to friends all over the world. It comes back to me and I send it out again.

Trust me—I mean nothing disrespectful toward those great cooks and companies out there who produce fabulous, fancy fruitcakes every year, some of them very expensive. But for the most part, fruitcakes have become known as one of those "under-appreciated" Christmas presents that no one knows what to do with (unless you happen to be someone who likes them!).

The truth is, no one likes to receive a gift that is worthless, not needed, or undesirable. God is history's greatest gift-giver who has never given a worthless gift to anyone. Think about the gifts God has given to mankind:

- His Son (John 3:16)
- Eternal life (Romans 6:23)
- The Holy Spirit (1 Thessalonians 4:8)
- Victory (1 Corinthians 15:57)
- Wisdom (Ephesians 1:17)

And that is just a short list—there are many more gifts God has given corporately. But did you know that God has given some gifts individually—unique gifts tailored specifically for each believer? In this lesson we are going to study the gifts of God to individual Christians.

In the last lesson, from verses 1–6 of Ephesians 4, we talked about unity. But as important as unity is on its own, it is seen most clearly when contrasted with diversity. The great strength of the body of Christ is unity, yet diversity. Each believer is called and gifted by God in a unique way. We celebrate each person's uniqueness as we celebrate our unity in Christ.

In verses 7–12 of Ephesians 4, we will see how God gives gifts to us and how we give them back to Him in service.

The Provision of Gifts to Individual Believers (4:7)

Paul begins with "but," which immediately sets up a contrast with what preceded. The contrast is between unity (verses 1–6) and diversity (verses 7–12).

The Gifts of God's Grace

The Bible is clear that God has given to every believer a spiritual gift—a divine ability to be used in serving the church for the glory of God. These God-given abilities are supernatural, originating in the grace of God, and are therefore different from our natural abilities and talents. They are also distinct from the fruit of the Spirit (Galatians 5:22–23). These gifts are distributed by the Holy Spirit "to each one individually as He wills" (1 Corinthians 12:11).

We will not go through all the individual gifts of the Holy Spirit in this lesson, but they are mentioned in three main passages in the New Testament: Romans 12, 1 Corinthians 12, and here in Ephesians 4. There are approximately 19 different gifts mentioned when you compile all the ones mentioned in these chapters. Every Christian has been given one or more of these gifts to accomplish something unique in the body of Christ. It's easy for some of us to think we don't have very unique talents, but no one should feel that way about spiritual giftedness since we are all recipients of God's grace-gifts.

The Grace of God's Gifts

Not only do we have the gifts of God's grace but we have the grace of God's gifts as well. We need His grace in order to use His gifts.

All of us have observed people who are highly gifted in the natural realm, but lack the grace and humility that makes their talent appreciated by others. The more talents a person has, the more grace they need—and the same is true with spiritual gifts. The more gifted a Christian is, the more grace is needed to use the gift(s) in a manner pleasing to the Lord and others. The Bible says God resists the proud but gives grace to the humble (James 4:6; 1 Peter 5:5).

Do you believe you are gifted by God? If you are a Christian you are gifted and graced by Him. You need to discover what His gift is and begin using it by His grace for His glory.

The Price of Gifts for Individual Believers (4:8-10)

Gifts are free to the recipient but costly to the giver. In the case of spiritual gifts, what we receive freely came at a high cost to God.

The Old Testament Promise (4:8)

Paul, the master teacher of the church, quotes a difficult passage from the Old Testament to make his point about the price of spiritual gifts (Psalm 68:18): "When He ascended on high, He led captivity captive, and gave gifts to men."

Paul's words are not a direct quote of the Old Testament passage, but he uses it as an analogy. It was a psalm with a celebration motif, picturing victorious armies returning from conquering a city. The returning soldiers would not only return with captives but all the spoils of war, the property, and valuables they had taken from the defeated city. They would also liberate any of their own soldiers who had been held captive by the defeated people. The victor would parade through his own city with prisoners of war, spoils of war, and liberated captives restored to freedom.

Paul uses this well-known motif to illustrate what Christ did. He came to earth and defeated our enemies: sin, Satan, and death. He was victorious over them all, then returned back to heaven as the conquering King and paraded before all the hosts of heaven with the spoils of war: "He led captivity captive." Colossians 2:14–15 tell us that Christ made a "public spectacle" of the principalities and powers He disarmed.

The New Testament Proof (4:9–10)

Paul now applies this Old Testament reference to Christ in the New Testament by asking, "'He ascended,' what does it mean but that he also first descended into the lower parts of the earth?"

This question of Paul's introduces one of the great mysteries of the Bible. What does it mean that Christ descended into the bowels of the earth? He could not have ascended to heaven if He had not first descended to earth, right? When He descended to earth, He came down to Bethlehem where He was born as a baby. But when He died, He descended even further—into the grave. But then He descended even further into Sheol where He declared the Gospel to the dead (stay with me on this!).

When Jesus was buried, His body was in the tomb but His spirit continued to live. Because of this passage, and 1 Peter 3:18–22, we believe that Jesus, between the time of His death and resurrection, went to Sheol (the place of the spirits of the Old Testament saints) and preached the Gospel to those who were there. If you recall, Jesus told the repentant thief on the cross, "Today you will be with Me in Paradise" (Luke 23:43). Paradise is not heaven. If is "half" of a region called Sheol where the spirits of the Old Testament dead resided: the righteous resided in Paradise and the unrighteous in

Hades. A chasm separated the two regions, as pictured in the story of Lazarus and the rich man (Luke 16:19–31).

When Christ went to Sheol and declared the message of His death on the cross, it was a message of despair and judgment for the unbelieving in Hades, but a message of celebration for the believing in Paradise. This is explained more fully in 1 Peter 3:18–20: "For Christ also suffered once for sins, the just for the unjust, that He might bring us to God, being put to death in the flesh but made alive by the Spirit, by whom also He went and preached to the spirits in prison, who formerly were disobedient, when once the Divine longsuffering waited in the days of Noah, while the ark was being prepared, in which a few, that is, eight souls, were saved through water."

After preaching to the souls in Sheol, Jesus took with Him to heaven the spirits of the righteous from Paradise when He Himself ascended to heaven. They became a great parade through the streets of heaven, the spoils of Jesus' victory at the Cross. Now Paradise is empty. Since the Cross, the spirits of the righteous dead go immediately to join Christ in heaven.

The phrase in verse 8, "gave gifts to men," refers to the celebration for the victory of Christ over sin, Satan, and death. The spiritual gifts God has given to us are celebratory gifts: free for us, but at the cost of His own life for Christ. He came to earth as God's representative to do battle against Satan. He returned victorious and now gives gifts to us in celebration of that victory, gifts that we now use to honor God in service to Him and to others.

Most Christians don't have a proper perspective on their spiritual gifts—they are not aware of all what went on behind the scenes in order to make the giving of those gifts possible. Like all gifts given sacrificially, our spiritual gifts have great value. They should be used humbly and for God's glory, not for ours.

THE PURPOSE OF GIFTS TO INDIVIDUAL BELIEVERS (4:11–13)

Now that we know where our gifts came from and at what cost, it's important to clarify the purpose of the gifts God has given us.

Gifts for the Foundation of the Church (4:11)

Christ's first gifts were for the foundation of the church: apostles, prophets, evangelists, and pastor-teachers (a dual gift; all pastors should be teachers, but not all teachers have to be pastors. There is a spiritual gift of teaching for those who are not pastor-teachers; Romans 12:7). Like the four corner pieces on a jigsaw puzzle which provide a frame for the rest of the pieces, so the four gifts mentioned here are foundational for the church.

1. The apostles

    Apostle means "sent one." These were the eleven original disciples (Judas excluded) plus Paul, in addition to others such as Barnabas, who are called apostles. Apostles had to be witnesses of the Resurrection, Paul's witness of the resurrected Christ coming at his conversion on the road to Damascus (Acts 9).

2. The prophets

    Prophets had two ministries: forthtelling (speaking forth the word of God) and foretelling (knowing the future by supernatural revelation).

3. The evangelists

    Evangelists went about preaching the good news of the Gospel, like Philip did (Acts 8:12, 26–40).

4. The pastor-teachers

    Pastor-teachers were those who shepherded flocks of Christians and taught them the Word of God.

Apostle and prophet are gifts no longer given in the church since Ephesians 2:20 says they were part of the foundation of the church. No one today has seen the risen Christ, and so cannot be a genuine apostle. These four were early gifts given to establish and shepherd the church, to build a strong foundation for the future.

Gifts for the Formation of the Church (4:12)

The purpose of the four foundational gifts was "for the equipping of the saints for the work of the ministry." Many pastors burn out early in their ministry because of misunderstanding this verse of Scripture. It doesn't say the gifts were given so pastors could equip the saints *and* do the work of the ministry. That would mean the pastor-teacher would be doing everything! I have actually had people early in my pastoral career tell me that I was being paid by the church to do the work of the ministry. That is the result of a complete misinterpretation of this verse.

The verse should be read so that the pastor-teachers equip the saints so that they (the saints) can do the work of the ministry. The *New Living Translation* says it well: "Their responsibility is to equip God's people to do His work and build up the church." The pastor's job is to teach and equip, and the members' jobs are to do the work of the ministry.

Even a proper understanding of the passage can be abused. This doesn't mean the pastor just shows up on Sunday and preaches and is invisible the rest of the week while the unpaid members are slaving away seven days of the week. Both the pastor and the members work together, equally diligent, but with different gifts and responsibilities so that the work of the ministry is accomplished.

The church is formed as the pastor-teacher equips the members who then "build up the church, the body of Christ."

Gifts for the Function of the Church (4:12b)

Gifts are given for two reasons, both of which relate to the functioning of the church: service and strengthening.

1. The Service of the Church

   Saints are equipped to do the work of the ministry, to serve the body of Christ. We did an audit at our church several years ago to discover just how many tasks it took to accomplish what we do on a weekly basis in our church. We discovered there were over 1,800 different volunteer tasks that needed to be performed, and I am sure the number is higher today than it was then.

   That's why God gives gifts of service and ministry to the church, to accomplish what needs to be done. Every Christian is to be employed in the service of God. We hear much about the unemployment rate in our economy, but it should be zero in the body of Christ because of the amount of work that needs to be done.

2. The Strengthening of the Church

   The work of the ministry is carried out in order to strengthen, or edify (build up) the church. Our gifts are like tools we each bring to the job site for building a house, only the structure is God's house, a temple of living stones, the church.

Two verses in closing: Romans 12:6 says with reference to our gifts, "let us use them." And 1 Peter 4:10 says, since we have received a gift, "minister it to one another." Our gifts are not toys to be trifled with or trophies to put on a shelf. They are the very essence of the grace of God to be used, to be put into service.

To the degree we don't use the gifts God has given us, to that degree the world sees a weak and anemic body of Christ. Conversely, the more we use our gifts, the stronger the house of God, the body of Christ, becomes in this world.

APPLICATION

1. To identify all the spiritual gifts mentioned in the New Testament, compare the three principal passages where gifts are listed. First, list the gifts from 1 Corinthians, then match the same gifts from Romans and Ephesians. Finally, number and list at the bottom of the Romans and Ephesians columns those gifts which don't appear in 1 Corinthians.

1 Corinthians 12:8–10, 28	Romans 12:6–8	Ephesians 4:11
1.		
2.		
3.		
4.		
5.		
6.		
7.		
8.		
9.		
10.		
11.		
12.		
13.		
14.		

Others from Romans: Others from Ephesians:

a. How many total gifts did you identify from the three passages?

b. What conclusions about the number of spiritual gifts can you arrive at in light of the lists not being the same in different New Testament epistles?

c. What reasons can you think of for a person having more than one gift? For having only one gift?

d. Are a person's gift(s) likely to be permanent, or could they change with the needs of a situation? Explain your answer:

e. What gifts does Peter mention in 1 Peter 4:10–11? Are these included in the lists above?

2. What spiritual gift(s) do you believe you have?

   a. How did you identify your gift(s)?

b. How are you using your gift(s) in the body of Christ?

c. What blessing or benefit have you noticed when you minister your gift(s) to others in the body?

d. How could you affirm the gifts of others who minister to you in the body of Christ?

e. What do you see as the primary negative result that comes from believers not using their spiritual gift(s)?

3. First Corinthians 12–14 are three chapters dealing with spiritual gifts in the church. How would you define the overall theme of each chapter? What is Paul communicating in each large section?

- Chapter 12

- Chapter 13

- Chapter 14

a. What is the primary message of 13:1–3?

b. Have you seen examples of people using their gift without grace (love)?

c. What is the net result between not using a spiritual gift and using it without love?

d. Which will last longer, love or spiritual gifts? (verse 13:8)

e. What single attitude on our part rules all other actions or attitudes? (verse 13:13)

DID YOU KNOW?

Spiritual gifts are tied by language to the grace of God. The Greek word in the New Testament for grace is *charis*, and the Greek word for spiritual gift is *charisma*, a grace-gift. There are other Greek words for gift besides *charisma*. *Doron* refers to gifts of honor like those the magi brought the Christ child (Matthew 2:11), and *dorea* refers to free gifts from God, like the gifts of Christ to the church (Ephesians 4:7). *Doma* focuses on the concrete nature of the gift itself, as in Ephesians 4:8. *Charisma* is always linked to a gift given by the grace of God, and is used primarily in the New Testament with reference to the gifts of the Holy Spirit to believers. Because spiritual gifts are not tangible, physical objects, some have referred to them as "gracelets" or "grace-gifts."

Turning Point
Resources
by Dr. David Jeremiah

The Blessings and Behavior of the Believer – Ephesians

Do you know that you have access to spiritual wealth? Begin to tap into your God-given riches with Dr. Jeremiah in his new study on the book of Ephesians. *The Blessings and Behavior of the Believer* invites you to discover the gifts God wants to give you, including a deeper relationship with Him and fellow believers. Learn how to live at your richest potential.

Study Guides

Volume 1 BBBSG1 *(Can-$14 / UK-£6)* $9
Volume 2 BBBSG2 *(Can-$14 / UK-£6)* $9

Cassette Albums

Volume 1 (10 tapes) BBBAL1 *(Can-$79 / UK-£33)* $50
Volume 2 (11 tapes) BBBAL2 *(Can-$86 / UK-£36)* $55

Compact Disc Albums

Volume 1 (10 CDs) BBBAL1CD *(Can-$110 / UK-£45)* $70
Volume 2 (11 CDs) BBBAL2CD *(Can-$121 / UK-£50)* $77

ORDER 1-800-947-1993

Turning Point
Resources
by Dr. David Jeremiah

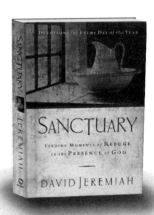

Sanctuary
Finding Moments of Refuge in the Presence of God

Dr. Jeremiah's first 365-day devotional will encourage you to maintain the awareness of God's manifest presence no matter where your day takes you. Each daily reading contains a Scripture passage and an insightful reflection for the day. Perfect for yourself or your next gift giving occasion, *Sanctuary* is beautifully packaged with a padded cover, original artwork throughout, and a ribbon page marker.

SANHBK 4" x 6" (Padded Cover Book—384 pages) *(Can-$22/UK-£9)* **$14**

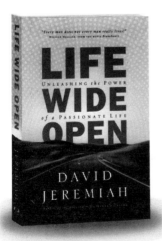

Life Wide Open
Unleashing the Power of a Passionate Life

Most Christians sense that something vital is missing from their walk with the Lord. We are easily discouraged and bogged down with busyness, boredom, mediocrity, and routine. In this energizing book, Dr. David Jeremiah opens our eyes to how we can live a life that exudes an attitude of hope and enthusiasm . . . a life of passion . . . a LIFE WIDE OPEN! *Life Wide Open* offers a vision, both spiritual and practical, of what our life can be when we allow the power of passion to permeate our souls.

LWOHBK (Hard Cover Book—206 pages) *(Can-$30/UK-£12.50)* **$19**

ORDER 1-800-947-1993

Turning Point Resources

STUDY GUIDES

All Study Guides are regularly priced at $9
An audiocassette album is also available for each of the following series.
(Sold separately. Individually priced.)

Authentic Christian Life, The
  (I Corinthians, 3 Volumes)
Bend in the Road, A (Psalms)
Blessings and Behavior of the Believer, The
  (Ephesians, 2 Volumes)
Celebrate His Love (Christmas)
Christians Have Stress Too
Christ's Death and Resurrection
Escape the Coming Night
  (Revelation, 4 Volumes)
Facing the Giants in Your Life
Family Factor
For Such a Time as This (Esther)
Fruit of the Spirit, The (Galatians)
Gifts from God (Parenting)
Giving to God
God in You (The Holy Spirit)
God Meant It for Good (Joseph, 2 Volumes)
Grace of Giving, The (Stewardship)
Greatest Stories Ever Told, The (Parables)
Handwriting on the Wall (Daniel, 3 Volumes)
Heroes of the Faith (Hebrews)
Home Improvement
How to Be Happy According to Jesus
  (The Beatitudes)
How to Live According to Jesus
  (The Sermon on the Mount, 2 Volumes)
Invasion of Other Gods (New Age)
Investing for Eternity
Issues of the Home and Family

Jesus' Final Warning (Prophecy)
Knowing the God You Worship
Learning to Live by Faith (Abraham,
  2 Volumes)
Living by Faith (Romans, 6 Volumes)
Looking for the Savior (Thessalonians,
  2 Volumes)
Miracles of Christ, The
My Heart's Desire (Worship)
Nation in Crisis, A (Joshua, 2 Volumes)
New Spirituality, The (New Age)
Overcoming Loneliness
People God Uses, The
People Who Met Jesus
Power of Encouragement, The
Power of Love, The
Powerful Principles from Proverbs
Prayer—The Great Adventure
Runaway Prophet—Jonah, The
Ruth, Romance, and Redemption
Seeking Wisdom—Finding Gold
Signs of the Second Coming
Spiritual Warfare
Stewardship Is Lordship
Ten Burning Questions from Psalms
Tender Warrior, The (David, 2 Volumes)
Turning Toward Integrity (James)
Turning Toward Joy (Philippians)
What the Bible Says About Angels
When Wisdom Turns to Foolishness (Solomon)

BOOKS

Bend in the Road, A (Psalms) $19
Escape the Coming Night (Revelation) $13
Gifts from God (Parenting) $19
God in You (The Holy Spirit) $19
Handwriting on the Wall, The (Daniel) $12
Jesus' Final Warning (Prophecy) $19
Life Wide Open (Purposeful Living) $19
My Heart's Desire (Worship) $19
Power of Encouragement, The $13

Prayer—The Great Adventure $19
Sanctuary (Daily Devotional) $14
Slaying the Giants in Your Life $19
Stories of Hope from a Bend in the Road $13
Things That Matter, The $10
Turning Toward Integrity (James) $10
Turning Toward Joy (Philippians) $10
What the Bible Says About Angels $13

BOOKLETS

*Creative Family Living: 20 Ideas for Christian
  Family Interaction* $6.50
Family Turning Points $6.50
Financial Turning Points $6.50
How to Encourage Your Children $2.50
Knowing God by Name $2.50
Living Right! 25 Behaviors of a Christian $6.50
Patriotic Turning Points $6.50
Powerful Prayer Promises $2.50

Plan for Whosoever, A $2.50
Prayer for Whosoever, A $2.50
Prophetic Turning Points $6.50
Signs at the Bend in the Road $2.50
Tour of Duty $4.00
Walking Down the Romans Road $2.50
Who I Am in Christ $2.50
Your Greatest Turning Point $2.50

POSTAGE AND HANDLING CHART	
For orders . . . . Add	
Up to $5.99	$1.50
$6.00-$19.99	$2.50
$20.00-$50.99	$3.50
$51.00-$99.99	$6.00
$100.00 & over	$9.00

If you would like a complete catalog
of resources available from
Turning Point, please call
1-800-947-1993 or write
Turning Point ~ P.O. Box 3838 ~
San Diego, CA 92163-1838.
You can also visit Turning Point at
www.turningpointonline.org